HERZOG

The Limits of Ideas

TWAYNE'S MASTERWORK STUDIES

Robert Lecker, General Editor

HERZOG

The Limits of Ideas

Jonathan Wilson

Twayne Publishers • Boston
A Division of G.K. Hall & Co.

Herzog: The Limits of Ideas
Jonathan Wilson

Twayne's Masterwork Studies No. 46

Published by Twayne Publishers
A Division of G. K. Hall & Co.
70 Lincoln Street
Boston, Massachusetts 02111

Copyediting supervised by Barbara Sutton
Book production by Gabrielle B. McDonald

Typeset in 10 point Sabon
by Compset, Inc. of Beverly, Massachusetts

Printed on permanent/durable acid-free paper
and bound in the United States of America

Library of Congress Cataloging-in-Publication Data

Wilson, Jonathan, 1950–
Herzog : the limits of ideas / Jonathan Wilson.
p. cm.—(Twayne's masterwork studies ; no. 46)
Includes bibliographical references
1. Bellow, Saul. Herzog. 2. Consciousness in literature.
I. Title. II. Series.
PS3503.E4488H4538 1990
813'.52—dc20 89-38928
CIP

0-8057-7996-5 (alk. paper). 10 9 8 7 6 5 4 3 2 1
0-8057-8045-9 (pbk.: alk. paper) 10 9 8 7 6 5 4 3 2 1

First published 1990

Contents

TO THE MEMORY OF
Harold Michael Shrier

Note on the References and Acknowledgments

I began this book with some fixed ideas about *Herzog,* having already written about the novel in another book. These ideas began to get revised after I had given a paper at the first Saul Bellow International Conference in Haifa and I would like to thank Alan Lelchuk and Martin Amis who put me straight on a number of issues. Larry and Susan Brink facilitated the writing of this text. I would also like to thank Robert Lecker for his patient stewardship of the book. As ever, the presence of my wife, Sharon Kaitz, and of my children, Adam and Gabriel, was powerfully sustaining.

All quotations from *Herzog* are from the first Viking Press edition (New York, 1964).

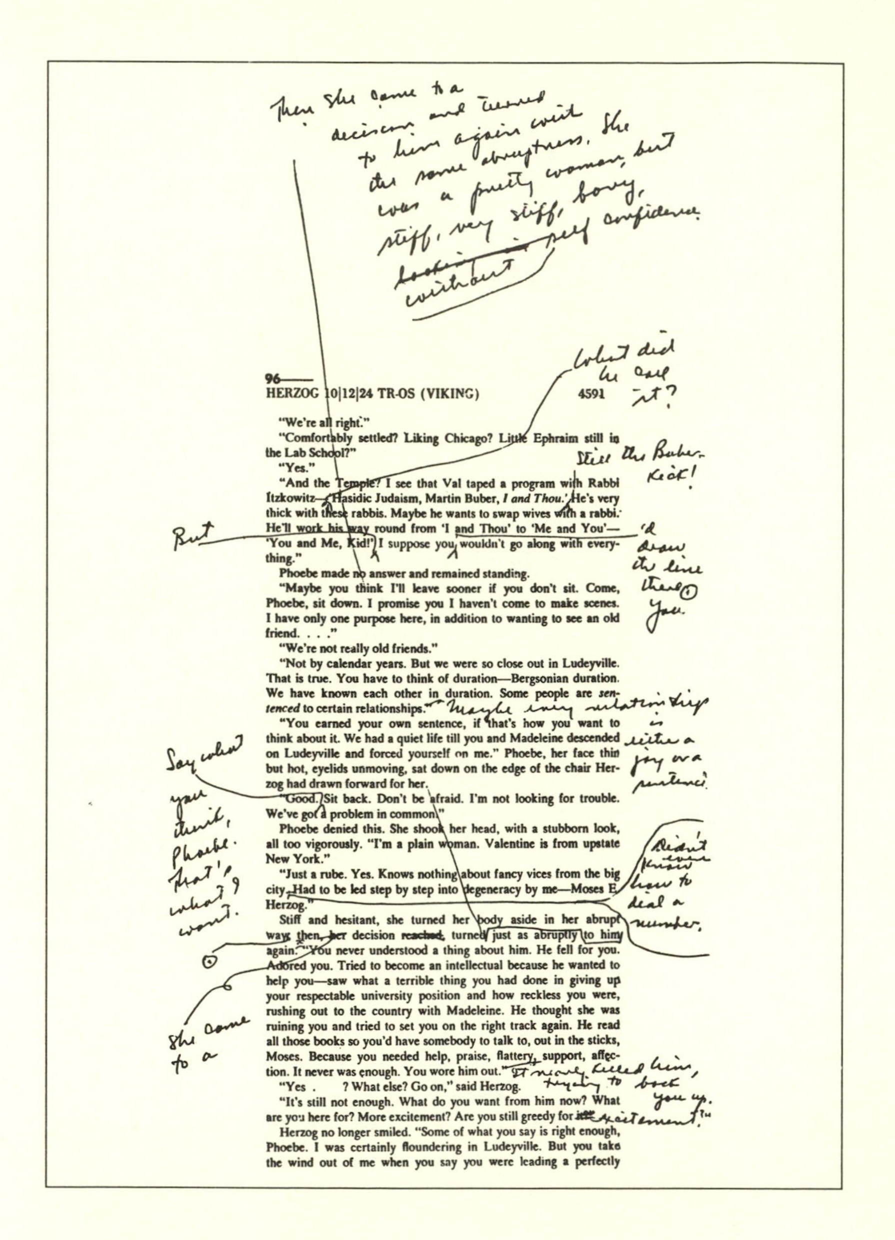

96——
HERZOG 10|12|24 TR-OS (VIKING) 4591

"We're all right."

"Comfortably settled? Liking Chicago? Little Ephraim still in the Lab School?"

"Yes."

"And the Temple? I see that Val taped a program with Rabbi Itzkowitz—'Hasidic Judaism, Martin Buber, *I and Thou*.' He's very thick with these rabbis. Maybe he wants to swap wives with a rabbi. He'll work his way round from 'I and Thou' to 'Me and You'—'You and Me, Kid!' I suppose you wouldn't go along with everything."

Phoebe made no answer and remained standing.

"Maybe you think I'll leave sooner if you don't sit. Come, Phoebe, sit down. I promise you I haven't come to make scenes. I have only one purpose here, in addition to wanting to see an old friend. . . ."

"We're not really old friends."

"Not by calendar years. But we were so close out in Ludeyville. That is true. You have to think of duration—Bergsonian duration. We have known each other in duration. Some people are *sentenced* to certain relationships."

"You earned your own sentence, if that's how you want to think about it. We had a quiet life till you and Madeleine descended on Ludeyville and forced yourself on me." Phoebe, her face thin but hot, eyelids unmoving, sat down on the edge of the chair Herzog had drawn forward for her.

"Good. Sit back. Don't be afraid. I'm not looking for trouble. We've got a problem in common."

Phoebe denied this. She shook her head, with a stubborn look, all too vigorously. "I'm a plain woman. Valentine is from upstate New York."

"Just a rube. Yes. Knows nothing about fancy vices from the big city. Had to be led step by step into degeneracy by me—Moses E. Herzog."

Stiff and hesitant, she turned her body aside in her abrupt way; then, her decision reached, turned just as abruptly to him again. "You never understood a thing about him. He fell for you. Adored you. Tried to become an intellectual because he wanted to help you—saw what a terrible thing you had done in giving up your respectable university position and how reckless you were, rushing out to the country with Madeleine. He thought she was ruining you and tried to set you on the right track again. He read all those books so you'd have somebody to talk to, out in the sticks, Moses. Because you needed help, praise, flattery, support, affection. It never was enough. You wore him out."

"Yes . ? What else? Go on," said Herzog.

"It's still not enough. What do you want from him now? What are you here for? More excitement? Are you still greedy for it?"

Herzog no longer smiled. "Some of what you say is right enough, Phoebe. I was certainly floundering in Ludeyville. But you take the wind out of me when you say you were leading a perfectly

Final galley proof of Herzog.
Courtesy of the Harriet Wasserman Literary Agency, Inc.

Chronology: Saul Bellow's Life and Works

1915	Saul Bellow born in Lachine, Quebec, 10 June (officially recorded as 10 July). The fourth child of Abraham and Liza (Gordon) Bellow, Saul is the first to be born after the family's emigration from St. Petersburg, Russia, in 1913. Spends early years in Canada in Montreal where his father works as an onion dealer and part-time bootlegger. Grows up hearing and speaking four languages: English, French, Hebrew, and Yiddish.
1924	Moves with family to Chicago, to the slums of the Northwest side.
1931–1933	Attends Tuley High School (now José de Diego High School) where 90 percent of the students are drawn from immigrant families.
1933	Enters the University of Chicago.
1935	Transfers to Northwestern University.
1937	Graduates from Northwestern with honors in sociology and anthropology. Enrolls in the University of Wisconsin where, on his own admission, he "behaves very badly," writing stories instead of working on his Ph.D. Marries Anita Goshkin during first Christmas break and does not return to the university. Makes decision "to become a writer." Birth of first son, Gregory.
1938–1942	Teaches at the Pestalozzi-Froebel Teachers college in Chicago. Works on WPA Writers' Project.
1941	Publishes first short story, "Two Morning Monologues," in *Partisan Review*.
1942	Moves to New York and lives in a modest apartment in Queens. Publishes "The Mexican General," also in *Partisan Review*.

1943	Works in the editorial department of the *Encyclopedia Brittanica* on the Great Books project.
1944	Publishes first novel, *Dangling Man*. Serves briefly in the merchant marine during World War II.
1946–1948	Teaches at the University of Minnesota in Minneapolis where he shares an office with John Berryman. Later Berryman dedicates *The Dream Songs* to Bellow and the two become colleagues again at Princeton. Publishes *The Victim* (1947).
1948–1950	Awarded a Guggenheim fellowship. Travels in Europe, and in 1950 returns to the United States, teaches evening courses at New York University, and becomes creative writing fellow at Princeton. "Sermon of Dr. Pep" (1949).
1951	"Looking for Mr. Greene"; "By the Rock Wall"; "Address by Gooley MacDowell to the Hasbeens Club of Chicago."
1952	National Institute of Arts and Letters Award.
1953	Publishes *The Adventures of Augie March*, which wins the National Book Award for fiction; translates Isaac Bashevis Singer's *Gimpel the Fool* from the Yiddish.
1953–1954	Teaches at Bard College. Lives at Tivoli in Duchess County, the "original" of the Berkshire setting in *Herzog*.
1955	Receives second Guggenheim fellowship. Spends some time on an Indian reservation in Nevada, where he writes *Seize the Day* and "A Father to Be."
1956	Publishes *Seize the Day*. Marries Alexandra (Sondra) Tschacbasov; a son, Adam, born of this marriage. "The Gonzaga Manuscripts."
1958	Receives Ford Foundation grant. "Leaving the Yellow House."
1959	Publishes *Henderson the Rain King*.
1960–1962	Co-edits *The Nobel Savage* with Keith Botsford and, for the first three issues only, Jack Ludwig. The magazine folds after five issues. Marries Susan Glassman in 1961; a son, Daniel, born of this marriage. Lecture tour through Europe and the Middle East. Becomes a member (and later chairman) of the prestigious Chicago Committee on Social Thought. Receives honorary doctor of letters from Northwestern University.
1963	Edits and writes introduction to *Great Jewish Short Stories*. Receives honorary doctor of letters, Bard College.
1964	Publishes *Herzog*, which wins his second National Book Award, the James L. Dow Award, the Fomentor Award, and Prix Internationale de Literature. *The Last Analysis* premieres

	at the Belasco Theatre on Broadway but closes after twenty-eight performances.
1965	Three one-act plays, "Out from Under," Orange Souffle," "A Wen," staged in April at The Loft on off-off Broadway under the general title *Under the Weather.*
1967	Covers Six-Day War as correspondent for *Newsday.* Much of the material turns up in *Mr. Sammler's Planet.* "The Old System."
1968	Publishes *Mosby's Memoirs and Other Stories.* Awarded the Croix de Chevalier des Arts et Lettres by the French government—the highest literary distinction given to noncitizens. Wins Jewish Heritage Award from B'nai B'rith.
1970	Publishes *Mr. Sammler's Planet.* Takes trip to Kenya and Uganda with Saul Steinberg.
1974	Marries Alexandra Bagdasar. "Zetland: By a Character Witness."
1975	Publishes *Humboldt's Gift,* which wins his third National Book Award and the Pulitzer Prize.
1976	Wins Nobel Prize for literature. Publishes *To Jerusalem and Back.*
1978	"A Silver Dish."
1979	Reports for *Newsday* on Sadat-Carter-Begin peace treaty signing in Washington, D.C.
1982	Publishes *The Dean's December.*
1984	Publishes *Him with His Foot in His Mouth and Other Stories.* Wins Malaparte Literary Award.
1987	Publishes *More Die of Heartbreak.* Attends and lectures at First International Saul Bellow Conference in Haifa, Israel.
1989	Publishes *A Theft.*

I

Historical Context

As a young writer Saul Bellow once described himself as a "Chicagoan, out and out,"[1] by which he meant to indicate that he was not an ivory tower type; but he has also described himself as someone who had "book-strained eyes"[2] by the age of seventeen, which suggests that, as a young man anyway, he must have spent almost as much time in the city of Chicago's libraries as on its streets. Bellow has kept on with his reading, just as he has remained an inveterate Chicagoan eager to share his fascination with and knowledge of the city.[3] Observing and participating in the life of the streets of Chicago and a life of reading are two modes of experience that on the surface appear antithetical but that have sustained and energized the imagination of Saul Bellow through a writing career that now spans almost five decades.

After forty-five years of critical attention, hardly a writer is left who has not been claimed as an influence on Saul Bellow: Melville, Whitman, Twain, Dreiser, Fielding, Blake, Swift, George Eliot, Joyce, Dostoyevsky, Gogol, Rabelais, Sholom Aleichem. I could go on and begin to incorporate all the orthodox thinkers, philosophers, and political scientists and all the cranky theosophists and dubious speculators in the metaphysical whose relationship with Bellow has been determined and examined. How can one writer possibly reveal so many influences? Bellow's critics may find patterns to fit their own agendas, but the breadth of Bellow's reading has manifested itself in diverse ways in his writing.

Bellow is one of our last great autodidacts, a member of the generation of Jewish-American intellectuals, including Philip Rahv, Lionel Trilling, and Delmore Schwartz, who came of age in the 1940s and who, even if they were attached for periods of time to universities, largely educated themselves outside institutional confines. They did it through reading, voluminously and fanatically. Times have changed. According to Bellow there has been in our time "a disheartening expansion of trained ignorance and bad thought. . . . we live in a thought world and the thinking has gone very bad indeed."[4]

In a talk he gave on "The Silent Assumptions of the Novelist"[5] Bellow addressed himself to the temptation that has always existed for American men of letters (and the specified gender is significant) to construct an unmediated relationship with American reality—to be "natural" writers. Bellow recalled a journey he had made in his early twenties, before he had written and published his first novel. He was on a train going through the Midwest on his way to visit an uncle. In his suitcase he had "more books than clothes." He was reading Nietzsche. He looked up from his book and gazed around at the other passengers. No one was reading anything. He thought, "How can they take America straight?" Without his books, he felt, he would not have survived. Since that time, of course, there are even more passengers on the train without a book in their hands, so much so that we might want to ask, Is anybody reading anymore?—reading, that is, in the insatiable fashion of Bellow and his contemporaries. One of the criticisms persistently leveled at successful young American fiction writers is that their work is conditioned not by a heightened consciousness of things present and books past but by the advertising media. The result, this criticism maintains, is a glitzy, stylish, and totally insubstantial body of fiction cozily entrenched either in a fashionable "dis-ease" or in a conscious or unconscious nostalgia for the suburban comforts of the late fifties and early sixties.

Bellow's work couldn't be more different. He is a novelist who writes through what he reads as much as through what he experiences. But this is not to say that Bellow's broad knowledge and rich erudition has turned his work into something dry and obscure. On the contrary, in his novels Saul Bellow has performed the remarkable feat of making an extraordinarily complicated mind accessible to a wide range of readers without compromising his thoughts through oversimplification. He has done this with the aid of the elastic form of the novel, a form that has allowed him to connect the rough, tough poetry of the Chicago streets on which he grew up with the thin air of erudite philosophical speculation and the trials and tribulations of domestic life—excruciating divorces, money woes—with the huge historical tragedies of our century, including the central fact of the Holocaust. Bellow is one of the few contemporary writers who has not underestimated either his audience's desire to grapple with big issues or its capacity to respond to an imaginative world peopled with characters who do a lot of deep thinking. It is surely significant that *Herzog*, a novel in which the protagonist writes mental letters to, among others, Heidegger and Nietzsche, spent many weeks on the *New York Times* best-seller list in 1964. This is not how things are supposed to go in America.

Bellow too is much more than the sum of his influences. Although we may want to point to the Dostoyevskian plots of his early novels, the Whitmanian exuberance and Dreiserian attention to detail in *The Adventures of Augie March*, or the Yiddish speech rhythms that sometimes direct the flow of Bellow's sentences, Bellow remains a writer who cannot be neatly categorized. Moreover, were we to read Bellow only through the prism of his own reading we would be getting less than half the picture. Although Bellow may be suspicious of the writer who *only* takes America straight (Erskine Caldwell is the example that Bellow himself offered in his talk), in his own life he has immersed himself, as perhaps no other contemporary novelist of his stature, in the rough and tumble of city life—the pulls, tugs, distractions, and attractions of urban American reality. Not for Bellow the conventional move to the countryside that accompanies literary success. Instead, he has preferred to remain in the heart of the city and, like one of his most recent heroes, Albert Corde, has thus opened himself up to "the inner city slum," which becomes "a material representation of the slum of the innermost being."[6]

The city of Chicago has been meat and drink to Bellow for sixty years, and like his Chicago heroes, Augie March, Moses Herzog, Charlie Citrine, and Albert Corde, Bellow seems familiar with both high life and low life, with professors and mobsters, political power figures and ex-cons, wealthy art-collecting widows and sleazy philistine lawyers. The culture of a city whose own relationship toward culture is more than passingly antagonistic has been one of Bellow's vitally explored subjects. In what was only partly a joke Bellow once took the podium at the annual Chicago Literary Arts Ball to express his "heartfelt sympathies to all Chicago writers"; after adding that "this is a tough town to be a writer in," he walked out—to a standing ovation. But although there may have been no "literary scene" in Chicago for most of Bellow's tenure as a citizen there, the unsmoothed surface and dynamic, sometimes violent, undercurrents of the city have intrigued and engaged Bellow, and they have directed his consciousness quite as powerfully as the library of his mind.

Bellow is fully American in his experience and European in some of his literary attachments, but he is also a Jewish writer, and although the generic classification Jewish-American fiction is, as Bellow himself has observed, ultimately reductive, there can be no doubt that Bellow's Jewishness and Jewish experience in this century inform much of his work. Bellow grew up hearing and speaking four languages, two of which were Yiddish and Hebrew (although the latter was "spoken" in the confines of the *cheder* and not the home or street). The heroes of his novels are almost exclusively Jewish and, as in *Herzog,* Bellow often, sometimes comically, sometimes poignantly, evokes the joys and miseries of a Jewish childhood spent first in the St. Dominick Street ghetto of Montreal (called Napoleon Street in *Herzog*) and from the age of nine in the slums of the Northwest side of Chicago. The Nazi Holocaust and the emergence and subsequent conflicts of the state of Israel are often on the minds of Bellow's heroes and, judging from his discursive prose and in particular his full-length work *To Jerusalem and Back,* on Bellow's mind as well.

An awareness of Bellow's background goes some way to explaining the proliferous mind of Moses Herzog, a mind that is sometimes staggering in the range of its thoughts and associations. But despite Bellow's ease in the world of ideas, his intentions are often to debunk the man who would live by ideas or books alone. Of *Herzog* he recently wrote, "Certain readers complained the book was difficult. Much as they might have sympathized with the unhappy and comical history professor, they were occasionally put off by his long and erudite letters. Some felt that they were being asked to sit for a difficult exam in a survey course in intellectual history, and thought it mean of me to mingle sympathy and wit with obscurity and pedantry. But I was making fun of pedantry!"[7] For Bellow "higher education" alone does not guarantee heightened insight into life's mysteries and certainly offers very limited education in the conduct of life—family matters, erotic needs. In these areas, says Bellow, "Herzog's confusion is barbarous."[8] Unlike his hero, Bellow has led the applied life. Taking his books with him wherever he goes, he has nevertheless not sat quietly in his study but rather ventured onto American streets, some of which are bright and some of which are very, very dark.

II

The Importance of the Work

Saul Bellow's *Herzog* was first published twenty-five years ago, not long enough yet, one might think, to grant it confidently the status of a classic. However, the novel's impact has been very great indeed, and its centrality to the work of a writer who is widely regarded as our one unarguably "major" contemporary American novelist demands that we pay attention.

The appeal of *Herzog*—and it is an odd book to have achieved such a broad readership—derives in part from Bellow's comic wit, discreet intelligence, powerful evocations of milieu, and entertaining characterizations, but more profoundly it seems to derive from the contemporary relevance of Moses Herzog's dilemmas. Bellow's hero is a man racked by domestic crises, unable to cope with the recent breakup of his marriage, plagued by his vindictive ex-wife, and betrayed by almost all of his friends. But although the folding of a middle-class marriage and all its unhappy constituents may be familiar territory to us, it is not only the social and psychological ramifications of divorce with which Bellow is concerned. Bellow is interested in the peculiar components of Western suffering. As he puts it, "We know the 'traditional forms of oppression' in the USSR. But we have a problem: What do people suffer from in the United States? We seem to say that unless we know the sufferings of people in a totalitarian state like the USSR, we don't really know what suffering and pain is. That's a mistake we make . . . —there is suffering here in the USA, in the West. . . . we have our ordeals here [too] . . . ordeals of privation . . . of desire."[9] Bellow is not equating the superficial heartbreak of a broken romance with the sufferings of the Gulag, but rather raising up for our serious attention what he calls "the suffering of freedom," suffering for which, unlike the acute suffering of the Gulag, we know no remedies. Such suffering is typified in the fate of Moses Herzog, a man who leads an unregulated, liberated life but who nevertheless feels himself to be in the grip of powers and forces that have rendered his personality and particularized individuality quite redundant.

Herzog is possessed of "*an unemployed consciousness,*"[10] and it is with the fate of this contemporary version of the Superfluous Man that Bellow is concerned. Herzog's marital crisis acts as a catalyst that sends his mind spinning in all directions. As we follow the raveling and unraveling of Herzog's brilliant, quirky, jokey, troubling, moving thoughts, we comprehend a character who in the range and complexity of his mind seems to grapple with a great many of the forces—historical, social, psychological, environmental—that impinge on the modern personality. The question, of course, is, What is the point of having all these wonderful thoughts flying around if they have nowhere to land? What is the smart, well-educated, thoughtful person to do in a culture that has no place for him or her? Herzog sees himself, on one level, as a man at odds with his time and with his country—a man whose trade is plumbing the soul of modern man in a place where his kind of plumbers have gone out of business. Herzog's America, a land of hard-nosed businessmen and hard-hearted politicians, tough-assed lawyers, and ice-cold alimony-grabbing women, has no time to listen to and in any case does not want to hear the "insights" of a Moses Herzog. Herzog, who in ancient Greece might have held an honored and valued public position or who might have played courtier/mage in the Renaissance, finds himself, in late twentieth-century America, confined to "the private realm." Of course, Bellow is making fun of Herzog and the rend in his being that reveals a sophisticated mind that cannot put back together the bits of broken life ("Who was there at the university to teach him how to deal with his erotic needs, with women, with family matters?"), but he is also drawing our sympathy toward the professor.

Herzog insists that there are truths to be discovered in the universe beyond the fashionably contemporary view that this is a dog-eat-dog world where only the ruthless survive, or a world where, given the bloody history of our time and the proliferation of cataclysmic weaponry, the only proper stance to adopt is nihilistic. Herzog does not run away from the evidence on the dark side that sometimes seems overwhelming and does not advocate quiescence or acquiescence; his response to his and our condition is complicated. But Herzog's affirmations of the endurance of valuable human qualities are all the more affecting because they come from a man who does not flinch from confronting all he knows of war and killing and suffering.

The importance of *Herzog* surely derives from the unusual stance that its protagonist adopts toward the vicissitudes of contemporary life. Herzog does not "escape" into drugs or mysticism or even into art, nor does he indulge or cultivate his despair; rather, he confronts and affronts both the materialist world where money is God and those literary and philosophical worlds where God is death and dread. Against these weltanschauungs Herzog offers the value of an achieved and successful life—a life that from the outside appears dilapidated but is shored up by sharp knowledge, deep emotion, rich thought.

Herzog continues to compel us not because of any simple optimism that bucks the trend but precisely because of the complexity of Herzog's affirmations. Herzog takes on a whole set of what he calls "Reality Instructors": writers, thinkers, figures in his daily life, people who think they know the world and how it operates and whose view is generally bleak. Those who provide the chastening "Lessons of the Real" range from the German existentialist philosopher Martin Heidegger to the Chicago divorce lawyer Sandor Himmelstein, from Herzog's Freudian analyst Dr. Edvig to his phony, sentimental, betraying "best friend" Valentine Gersbach. Herzog struggles to come to terms with domestic banality, sexual betrayal, a lack of public place, a country that seems to have lost its values and traditions, a world violent and crazy—a life, in fact, that many of the great thinkers and artists of the century have concurred in thinking is quite pointless. Herzog does not emerge unscathed from his skirmishes with reality, but we read the book, perhaps, to discover that there are indeed some truths on the side of life.

III

Critical Reception

> My novel deals with the humiliating sense that results from the American mixture of private concerns and intellectual interest. That is something which most readers of the book seem utterly to have missed. . . . To me, a significant theme of *Herzog* is the imprisonment of the individual in a shameful and impotent privacy. He feels humiliated by it; he struggles comically with it; and he comes to realize at last that what he has considered his intellectual "privilege" has proved to be another form of bondage. Anyone who misses this misses the point of the book.[11]

Thus Saul Bellow, answering an interviewer's question about Herzog in May 1965, just a year after the novel's publication. The double bind of the intellectual man who is full of great ideas that have nowhere to go and thus circulate around the thinker, enmeshing him in his own thought figures; the painful irony and dark humor of an American life given over to an education that does many things for the mind but does not offer instruction in the conduct of life—these are Bellow's declared subjects in *Herzog*. However, since its publication the novel has engaged critics and readers alike in such a broad area of commentary and response that Bellow's early insistence that there was a "point" not to be missed now appears unnecessarily reductive and perhaps most interesting in the way that it exemplifies the powerful attempts that authors make to control interpretation of their own texts.

When it first appeared in 1964 *Herzog* caused a stir; the early reviews were overwhelmingly laudatory, with some reviewers going so far as to claim the novel as an "instant classic." There was an unmistakable exuberance in the reviews of *Herzog* as if feelings long dormant found in the novel a catalyst to awaken them and were now being expressed for the first time. This may sound like a vague description of concrete critical activity, but Bellow's early readers seemed hardly to know themselves what they found so appealing about the novel.

George Elliott, writing in the *Nation,* came closest to identifying the liberating principle behind the euphoria when he described Moses Herzog as "the first intellectual in American fiction whose mind is fully a part of him, who is all there in the reader's imagination." He went on to assert that "after *Herzog* no writer need pretend in his fiction that his education stopped in the eighth grade."[12] While poking fun at pedantic intellectuals and underscoring the inadequacy of "ideas" as panaceas for domestic woes, Bellow nevertheless simultaneously legitimizes the complex mind of an intellectual as proper fare for the American novel. He enriches a novel that, in the twentieth century, had largely predicated itself on a hidden or not-so-hidden anti-intellectualism and many of whose most established practitioners (Philip Rahv's "redskins," for example—Caldwell, Dreiser, Hemingway, Lewis, Saroyan, Steinbeck), however bookish they may have been in their lives, nevertheless in their work and in their public personas presented a cultivated nonchalance toward ideas and the life of the mind.

Bellow's novel was acclaimed by an intellectual community that until *Herzog* had sensed itself as a beleaguered, peripheral, perhaps even an emasculated group, whose vibrant love of literature was perceived by the culture as a whole as dry cerebrality and whose reflective, bibliocentric reader's worlds hardly excited the imagination in the same way as the supposedly rich experiential words of the adventurous American novelist. Unlike the critic at home with his books, the Great American Novelist always seemed to be out getting in touch with the land and the people, or covering a war, or hunting or boxing or catching tarpon. With *Herzog*, much to his audience's delight, Bellow finally filled the prescription for a new fiction that he had written for himself on the first page of his first novel, *Dangling Man*.

> Today, the code of the athlete, of the tough boy—an American inheritance I believe from the English gentleman—that curious mixture of striving, asceticism, and rigor . . . is stronger than ever. Do you have feelings? There are correct and incorrect ways of indicating them. Do you have an inner life? It is nobody's business but your own. Do you have emotions? Strangle them. To an extent everyone obeys this code. . . . But on the truest candor, it has an inhibitory effect. Most serious matters are closed to the hard-boiled. They are unpracticed in introspection, and therefore badly equipped to deal with opponents whom they cannot shoot like big game or outdo in daring.[13]

By contrast, the hero of Bellow's novel was going to blab, to intellectualize, and he wasn't going to feel "guilty of self-indulgence." For most critics, however, Bellow's Joseph, the hero of *Dangling Man*, never quite materialized as the Hemingway-bashing alternative that he promised to be, but Moses Herzog did. As one critic affirmed, one of the chief reasons for the success of *Herzog* in the intellectual community was the fact that it demonstrated "that the life of the mind can in fact be as important and exciting a source of creative vitality as the life of the groin."[14]

The sense of vindication felt throughout the nation's humanities faculties and English departments was not altogether groundless but nevertheless rested on a prejudiced reading of the novel. This reading failed to take into account not so much the anxiety that surrounded Moses Herzog's own intellectuality—the "mixed blessing" of high cultural expertise and practical inefficiency—but rather the fear subtly threaded into the novel that to be an intellectual is indeed to court emasculation. Bellow perhaps did not stray as far from Hemingway as had been imagined. For Herzog, who paints and sprays and hammers and who likes to "play Chicago tough guy," seems sensitive to the notion that his functionless life may indeed take place "in the female realm," and both he and Bellow appear concerned to demonstrate that the life of the mind is not concomitant with the life of a wimp.

If *Herzog* brought American intellectuals out of the closet, it also firmly established the centrality to American fiction of Jewish-American writing. Julian Moynihan, reviewing *Herzog* on the front page of the *New York Times Book Review* wrote, "Over the past ten or fifteen years, Jewish writers . . . have emerged as the dominant movement in our literature. *Herzog* in several senses is the great pay-off book of that movement."[15] *Herzog* thus consolidates a shift in the demographics of American fiction that had slowly been occurring since the end of World War II. Paradoxically, the new American literary establishment in the sixties was largely comprised of minority writers, with Jewish and black writers particularly prominent—we might think of James Baldwin, Ralph Ellison, Norman Mailer, Bernard Malamud, Philip Roth, and J. D. Salinger along with Bellow. It is within this context that Moses Herzog could emerge as a powerfully representative American man, a contemporary version, as so many of the first reviewers noted, of Joyce's Leopold Bloom.

In *Herzog* we have Bloomsday as Herzog's week, and it is no accident that the only Jewish character other than Bloom to appear in *Ulysses* is none other than a Moses Herzog. The experience of Dublin life that courses through Leopold Bloom's mind like an ocean rushing through a sponge became, in its Bellovian incarnation, the familiar but overwhelming distractions of American urban life that must be apprehended, sorted, and thought through. Like so many of his fellow citizens (and unprotected by his intellectual advantage), Herzog must face the crime and violence spawned by New York and Chicago, but he must also deal with the power mongers on the other side of the stockade—willful lawyers, overbearing businesspeople, shrinks, clerics, and corrupt politicians. At the center of Herzog's problems is his disintegrating marriage and consequent failures at work and difficulties of renewed commitment in love.

However, despite his "every-middle-class-man" appearance, what really makes Moses Herzog so engaging a figure is that in contrast to the literary fashion of the previous decade his experience does not lead him down paths of nihilism. When Moses Herzog suffers, unlike the heroes of Camus, Sartre, or Beckett, he "suffers in style." One of *Herzog*'s first reviewers chose to describe Bellow's protagonist not as a contemporary Bloom but rather as a "Pierre Bezhukov of the thermonuclear society."[16] However, while like Melville's hero, Herzog is beset on all sides by the cynical and unsympathetic cruelties of society, unlike Pierre, Herzog refuses to sink into disillusion. With his wit intact and his faith, which he shares with his creator, that "there are some truths on our side in the universe," Herzog is able to distance himself from his own struggles and pains and take some pleasure in the social comedy in which he performs.

The "optimism" of the novel—a tempered optimism, to be sure—nevertheless was felt by some critics to be unearned and unjustified. The first dissenting voices in the chorus of praise that *Herzog* received on its publication came from critics who found Bellow's vision to be unhealthily accommodating of the social and political status quo. John W. Aldridge described the novel as "heaving a fatty sigh of middle-class intellectual contentment" and characterized Bellow's hero as "arrogantly complacent in his new found affirmative position."[17] Richard Poirier read Herzog's "affirmations" as lip service to a position that Bellow wished to endorse but that the novel itself flagrantly contradicted; "the novel," he wrote, "works as a rather conventional drama of alienation, though this is precisely what Bellow doesn't want it to be."[18] Reading through the early reviews of *Herzog,* though, the discovery is quickly made that whatever the reservations, criticisms, and judgments, the general sense conveyed is that Bellow's is the most compelling voice in American fiction. "Saul Bellow is the most rewarding of living American novelists," wrote V. S. Pritchett, "he remains for me even in *Herzog* [not a Pritchett favorite] the most distinguished and interesting American novelist."[19] This kind of "he's the best we have" criticism, which has remained a trope of Bellow criticism ever since the publication of *Herzog,* did not really do much to explain just what it was about *Herzog* that set Bellow apart, but it is exemplary of the general euphoria that greeted *Herzog,* a novel clearly destined to be a seminal American work.

The second stage of *Herzog* criticism began a year after the novel's publication when the British critic Tony Tanner published the first full-length study of Bellow's fiction. In Tanner's view, *Herzog* was the book that Bellow had been heading toward for twenty years—the novel that seemed "to summarize and contain all the questions, the problems, the feelings, the plights and the aspirations worked over in the previous novels.[2]' Tanner found Moses Herzog to be both a singularly American literary type and simultaneously a representative modern mind (perhaps the most compelling representative that contemporary culture had yet given us), and Herzog was recognizably a product of American literature in the dynamic conflicts that he enacted between his ideas and his behavior. For Tanner, Herzog was a late-coming incarnation of the American hero we have known since the middle of the nineteenth century, a character, always male, who desires fixity—in the form of home, wife, family, the cultivated comforts of city life—but who, fearing that stasis is synonymous with paralysis and that responsibility is potentially deathly, opts for "flow"—down the river, out onto the ocean, or lightly over the borders into the territories. The thoroughly modern Herzog is similarly caught: stressing the value of relationships he contrives to spend most of his time alone and insulated; dreaming of true community he finds himself in flight from society. But Herzog is also set apart from his forbears by his uniquely modern predicament. Unlike Huck or Ishmael, Herzog is reduced to an experience that is largely verbal. He is also besotted with information, ideas, and theories and compulsively driven to use the systems of thought bequeathed him by a contemporary education to "explain" everything that happens both to him and the world around him. In this sense, Tanner found Herzog's disease to be also "his age's."[21]

Tony Tanner was the first of many critics to recognize the way in which Bellow had used Herzog's oscillating consciousness to convert his personal crisis into the more impersonal crisis of modern thinking. However, in suggesting, as he did, that Herzog's thoughts were "mismanaged and patternless,"[22] Tanner appeared to imply that if Herzog's life was the objective correlative of the ills of the culture it was of its randomness and ungraspability. Although later critics have agreed that Herzog's apparently wild and spontaneous outbursts of thought on all manner of public issues relate at almost every point to Herzog's own troubled life, they take pains to stress those aspects of Herzog's personality that are ideationally set against both the myths and the reality of contemporary cultural disintegration. In the hands of critics like Gabriel Josipovici and Malcolm Bradbury the novel that, like Herzog's thinking, Tony Tanner found "patternless" emerges as structurally integrated in a manner paradigmatic of Herzog's thought. Bellow not only took great care with his form (there are six thousand pages of original *Herzog* manuscript) but also gave Herzog a very clear line to push. Herzog's "line," which is discussed further in chapters 5 and 6, might be paraphrased as meliorist, liberal humanist, skeptical romantic. Herzog's enemies in the fields of philosophy and literature are proponents of what he calls "the Wasteland outlook"—nihilists and existentialists; in psychology the opposing forces comprise dogmatic Freudian epigones; in religion they are Calvinist; in politics, Marxists. Herzog is suspicious of anyone, in fact, who offers a closed system of thought for understanding the world or who views life from an unremittingly determinist standpoint.

The job of unraveling and synthesizing Herzog's own multifarious ideas seems to have been taken on piecemeal over the last twenty-five years, with critics illuminating a particular aspect of Herzog's thought—one attending to Herzog and history, another to Herzog and transcendence, a third to Herzog and optimism, and so on. Recently, however, the critic Daniel Fuchs has provided the novel's readers with the first truly exhaustive account of Herzog's intellectual milieu.[23] Fuchs fully extrapolates and contextualizes the myriad theories with which Herzog grapples and attends in particular to Herzog's polemical thrust against "the absurd" and his ambivalent relation to Romanticism and the tenets of its modernist offshoots. Fuchs also takes on Bellow's slippery and complex relationship with Freud, revealed in *Herzog* in the protagonist's respectful but skeptical approach to Freud himself and simultaneous derisive scorn for contemporary psychoanalysts. For Herzog, it is dangerous to view the unconscious as yet another inescapably deterministic force. In the Freudian formulation we are "done in" by sexual impulses we will never understand. Herzog, and Fuchs suggests Bellow too, does not like to think that what a man thinks he is doing counts for nothing. Problematically, however, for the success of Herzog's and Fuchs' arguments the novel itself actually seems to embody rather than contradict Freudian ideas, in particular the way in which Herzog's highly energized ideas are presented as sublimations of his sexual frustrations and anger.

For the most part, perhaps because he is a writer of more or less traditional fictions, Bellow has attracted the attention of more or less traditional critics. Unfortunately, as far as *Herzog* is concerned, the result has been a homogeneous response to the novel. The overriding concern of the majority of *Herzog* critics in the last two and a half decades seems to have been to pry out the mechanisms of Bellow's unseasonable affirmations and display them for our edification. The result has been a litany of familiar claims as to the "life-affirming" qualities of Bellow's fiction. As one critic has suggested, the "comfortable orthodoxy" that seeks to confirm Bellow as the last level-headed humanist in a world gone mad for apocalypse has recently been threatening to "harden into dogma."[24] The titles of some of the full-length works to have appeared on Bellow's fiction are powerfully suggestive of the bias: *Saul Bellow: In Defense of Man; Saul Bellow: Quest for the Human; Whence the Power? The Artistry and Humanity of Saul Bellow.* Bellow's vision is at once more troubled and complicated than is commonly supposed. The occasional sense of "unearned gladness"[25] that Tony Tanner felt crept into *Herzog* is suggestive of an issue in the novel that must be confronted: Is Herzog's "optimism" conjured out of airy nothing, as often he seems to "affirm" against the evidence of his own experience? What are the grounds of Herzog's ultimate serenity and good humor? Have they been achieved by the hero or merely willed by the author?

By contemporary standards, of course, these questions with their hermeneutically inspired phrasing sound irremediably old-fashioned.

In the last few years students of literature and literary criticism have become much more familiar with the formulations of Roland Barthes, Jacques Derrida, Harold Bloom, Paul De Man, and others than with the predominantly "new critical" approach of the Bellow critics. However, the burgeoning of literary theory in our time—a theory that in the case of deconstruction is increasingly unchallenged (partly because it posits itself as unchallengeable)—makes a novel like *Herzog*, which predicates itself on its own "uncertainty principle" (Moses Herzog regards self-perpetuating, all-embracing thought systems with deep suspicion), all the more pertinent and valuable. Herzog, for example, is eager to repudiate Freudian determinisms but is aware that opponents of Freud are quickly characterized by Freudians as exhibiting symptoms of "resistance." Similarly, critics who resist deconstruction are characterized by deconstructionists as merely revealing the depths of their anxieties about a literary theory that they have not grasped—and most important, what they have not grasped is the self-subverting nature of the theory. Would Moses Herzog have embraced deconstruction as a theory subversive of the closed systems of thought that he abjured, or would he have regarded it as yet another theoretical net in which a person can be trapped? Again, the answer to such a speculative question, centered on character, probably is not to be found in the works of the most recent and radical critiques of *Herzog*.

Belatedly, Bellow's texts themselves have now become the subject of structuralist and deconstructionist inquiry. The first extensive structuralist and psychoanalytic examination of Bellow's fiction—Claude Levy's *Les Romans de Saul Bellow: Tactiques Narratives et Strategies Oedipiennes*—was published in France in 1983, and more recently in an as yet unpublished talk the Israeli critic William Freedman has attempted to deconstruct Bellow's fiction.[26] These new approaches to Bellow's writing can only revitalize a critical inquiry into Bellow's fiction, which had been threatening to dissolve into intellectual complacency.

There have now been well over a hundred scholarly articles and book chapters devoted to Saul Bellow's *Herzog*. The text continues to inspire and excite readers as a source of pleasure, argument, and discussion.

a reading

IV

In the Female Realm

> To look for fulfillment in another, in interpersonal relationships, was a feminine game. And the man who shops from woman to woman, though his heart aches with idealism, with the desire for pure love, has entered the female realm. (188)

What happens in *Herzog*? A man, Moses Herzog, spends a week and a half in feverish thought going over the breakup of his most recent marriage (his second) and all its contingent elements: betrayals, lies, affairs, child-custody problems, alimony payments, yearnings for revenge. Almost all of the action of the novel takes place inside Herzog's head, cast as memory, fantasy, reflection, philosophical speculation, and, most entertainingly, as a series of mental letters written to the living and the dead. For the most part, Herzog finds a good place to do his thinking—couch, bed, or hammock—but the exigencies of Bellow's plot also call for him to move around. For the first two-thirds of the novel Herzog travels aimlessly—from New York to Martha's Vineyard and back. In the last third he flies to Chicago with the avowed intention of murdering his ex-wife, Madeleine, and her lover Valentine Gersbach. He doesn't go through with it, which comes as no surprise at all to the reader. At the end of the novel Herzog has found his way to his run-down old country house in the Berkshires. We leave him as we have found him, lying on a couch, thinking.

The excitements of thought—highly charged thought, complex intellectual formulations, deep emotional reflections—form the substance of Bellow's narrative, and the issue of high-powered evocative thinking—Why does Herzog do so much of it? What is its use?—is at the thematic center of the novel.

The playwright David Mamet was asked in a recent interview where he got his ideas; Mamet replied, "I think of them." The bland immateriality of thinking—Mamet pointedly did not say "from books" or "from things that have happened to me" or even "from my imagination"—is not something that is high on our culture's list of priorities. We value action, and people who devote a lot of time to apparently purposeless thought we call "eggheads" or "space cadets": they are not here with the rest of us.

Not all thought is disparaged in our society, of course. If it has to do with curing cancer or launching space-shuttles, we are likely to be in awe of it. Or if it is useful thought with a clear application and a societally endorsed financial reward, we can respect it. But thoughts like Moses Herzog's—distracted ruminations on a seemingly endless variety of topics, inspired by a yearning to restore some measure of meaning to lives that have gone flat—are not generally considered to hold much of value for anyone save the thinker himself. Herzog has no institutional outlet where he can express his ideas: he is not a priest or rabbi with a congregation, and he is no longer a practicing professor with an audience of students.

Herzog, so he tells us, "craves use" (308), and for a while in his life he entertained the notion that he had one—believing that his thinking and writing could indeed contribute to a radical shift in consciousness. In his current state, unemployed, not writing but simply thinking, Herzog has had to put such vain ambitions aside. But the question remains, given his talents, "Who can make use of him?" (308). Herzog feels that he has no place or has lost his place in the world of men. The gender is significant for, like so many of Saul Bellow's unorthodox intellectual heroes, Herzog feels that, against his will, he has been obliged to enter "the female realm." The female realm is where thoughts that "don't matter" may circulate with freedom and ease, and where everything that is private, interior, and individual may be celebrated. The female realm, as we shall see, is also a hideout for Romantic philosophers and erotic enthusiasts. What it means to be "confined" there is of primary concern to both Herzog and Bellow.

There are a lot of women in Moses Herzog's life—middle-aged and old, ex-wives, lovers, the mothers and aunts of his ex-wives and lovers, an aged stepmother, the wife of his ex-wife's lover, women who are simply friends, and more. When Moses Herzog is not with a woman, he often is thinking about one—remembering an affair, recalling a visit with a cantankerous old aunt, being haunted by the powerful memory of his loving, soft, self-martyring mother, or imagining, in a variety of ways, the exacting revenge that he will take on Madeleine Pontritter, the ex-wife who has done him most wrong.

With the exception of his current lover, Ramona Donsella, who runs a flower shop on Lexington Avenue, none of Herzog's women have jobs. The old ones sit at home and conspire, and the middle-aged women dabble in a variety of studies, never applying themselves for very long or with any particular goal in sight. What really interests Herzog's women is the world of personal relationships: erotic life and what Herzog calls "hugging and heartbreak" (94). Some women, like Tennie and Zelda (Madeleine's mother and aunt), betray Herzog, whereas others, like his overseas lovers Wanda and Zinka, give him succor. From some women Herzog gets hugs and from others heartbreak. However, whether he is in the arms of the sexually restorative Ramona or the clutches of the castrating Madeleine, Herzog's main question to himself, throughout the novel, seems to be something along the lines of, "What am I doing hanging around with all these women? Isn't there something better, more productive, more valuable to the larger public world, that I should be putting my time into?"

Does this sound, to the contemporary ear, like boorish sexism? On the surface, it does. The world that Bellow has given Herzog to inhabit is a place where women "do" very little—where all the lawyers, businesspeople, doctors, shrinks, and high-powered academics are men. Of course, the sociological realities of early 1960s America were somewhat different from our own, but in any case, it is not really the "jobs" that they do that hierarchically separate the women from the men in Herzog's scheme of things. In fact, in *Herzog,* the world of professional labor is not elevated above the world of personal entanglement. When Moses Herzog despairs of "the female realm," it is only because he is experiencing a yearning to enter a realm that no longer exists.

"The occupation of a man," Herzog tells us, "is in duty, in use, in civility, in politics in the Aristotelean sense" (94). The key word here is *Aristotelean.* Herzog would like to live Aristotle's *bios politikos* in which the philosopher may devote himself to public political matters—not to those areas of political life that are down and dirty, like the placating of interest groups or the management of sewer systems—but to the contemplation of human affairs and of how best to establish and sustain them at their highest level. Herzog feels the same frustration as a Greek citizen of the *polis* who has been confined to the private sphere—that is, literally, the realm outside the inner wall of the city that is inhabited, day and night, by slaves, craftsmen, and women, all of whom are, in one way or another, imprisoned by *labor.* The difference for Herzog is that in contemporary America, as opposed to ancient Greece, labor, in all its forms, has jumped the fence and become not only respectable but also the standard by which we measure achievement. For us, work is a value in and of itself. What is more, there are no more philosophers of the type Herzog would like to be. Even those who in our own century have resembled, vaguely, Athenian philosophers—that is, the "political advisers" who have surrounded a president—have long ago been replaced by image makers and technocrats. Herzog, living in a century where "*those who think a great deal . . . effect nothing, and those who think nothing evidently do it all*" (66), thus finds himself in what he chooses to call "the female realm." This female realm is inhabited largely, but not exclusively, by women and is synonymous, in Herzog's mind, with "private life." Herzog's confinement to the female realm is intimately related to his feelings of ineffectuality in the larger world and to his deep ambivalence about those feelings.

Moses Herzog is a professor who has abandoned a promising teaching career in order to devote himself more concentratedly to the life of the mind. His intention was to produce a block-busting book on Romanticism, but the disintegration of his second marriage has interrupted his work and is beginning, he feels, to do him in as well. When we first apprehend him in the novel, Herzog's occupation appears to be making sense of his life so far and attempting to understand how he has arrived in his present parlous state. To these ends, Herzog, being the contemporary personality that he is, lies down on a couch in his Manhattan apartment and, in an act of parodic analysis, recalls and recapitulates the formative moments of his life: dramatic, comic, tender, violent, and moving. From time to time Herzog gets up and goes out into the world. For the most part he journeys to destinations that he abandons almost as soon as he has arrived, but wherever he is, in a taxi-cab, on a train or plane, swinging in a hammock, or simply delivering a monologue to a sympathetic listener, the self-analysis continues unabated.

The particular task that Herzog has set himself is to track down the roots of the breakup of his marriage to Madeleine Pontritter and to exorcise her demonic presence from his mind. In more general terms, however, Herzog's therapeutic recovery of Madeleine in memory (in the belatedly acknowledged hope, of course, of recovering himself) becomes a platform for the contemplation of a more public crisis: the crisis of consciousness in contemporary America, a place where "people can be free . . . but the freedom doesn't have any content" (39). The situation, Herzog tells us, is serious; "People are dying—it is no metaphor—for lack of something real to carry home when day is done" (28).

It is paradoxical that women, who have been kept out of "public life" for so long, should now have the fullest understanding of what to do to create a fulfilling private life. "Private life"—once considered a form of servitude and still experienced by Herzog, in his more self-glorifying moments, as somehow degrading—has, in contemporary democratic society, become both the given and the goal. "The revolutions of the twentieth century, the liberation of the masses by production, created private life" but, Herzog insists, "gave nothing to fill it with" (125). Herzog's women do have various strategies for turning private life into something meaningful but, unfortunately for Herzog, none that he can wholeheartedly embrace.

Herzog's most persuasive instructor is his lover Ramona. A sexy, kindhearted woman in her late thirties, Ramona, tuning into the zeitgeist (her female wisdom is not ancient), has turned herself into a priestess of the "Mystical Body" (202). Ramona keeps Norman O. Brown's *Life against Death* and Herbert Marcuse's *Eros and Civilization* on her bedside table and, like her gurus, she asserts the claims of desire, pleasure, and unconsciousness.

An educated woman, Ramona nevertheless likes to come on "like one of those broads in a girlie magazine" (202). With her black lace underwear and three-inch spiked heels, Ramona does her best to convince Herzog that the rejuvenation of his (and all) low spirits can come only through the body. Herzog, however, although in no doubt that he enjoys Ramona's company—and going to bed with her—nevertheless remains suspicious: "But is this the secret goal of my vague pilgrimage? Do I see myself to be after long blundering on unrecognized son of Sodom and Dionysus—an Orphic type? . . . A petit bourgeois Dionysian?" (17). First, Herzog is put off by any theory that makes too large a claim on life, and in this sense, the revolutionary theorists that have influenced Ramona are no more appealing to Herzog than the orthodox thinkers whom they challenge—psychoanalysts who champion the unrepressed terms in the Freudian oppositions of consciousness versus unconsciousness, ego versus id, and reality versus pleasure. Second, Ramona herself is clearly tired, putting on an act somewhat, desperate for a husband and committed to sex as a way of getting one. By observing Ramona carefully, Herzog comes to see that private life as an unending erotic carnival looks like fun but isn't.

Other women have also had ideas for straightening out Herzog. One of his former girlfriends, Sono Oguki, has already offered him a similar, although slightly less programmatic, way out of his confusion.

Sono calls Herzog her "professeur d'amour" (172) (Sono is Japanese, but their relationship is conducted in French), but, like Ramona, it is Sono who comes up with the new ideas. Sono's way is also that of the body, but hers has a luxurious and ceremonial oriental overlay. A lot of bathing and preening goes on in the Herzog/Sono relationship. Sono dresses Herzog in a kimono, brings him small cups of tea to slake his thirst, and presents him with erotic scrolls to whet his appetite. Herzog feels as if he is Sono's "concubine," and as with Ramona this is part of the problem. Like so many of Saul Bellow's heroes, Herzog is malleable, passive in his relationships, and always willing to go along with the other person's schemes—at least until such time as the new life that is being offered to him starts to feel like a form of bondage. Sono's concern and desire to please, her sexual and emotional altruism (she does not demand anything from Herzog except that he turn up at her place with a certain regularity, and in this he fails her miserably), only remind Herzog that he is incapable of making such a commitment to love life—although love life seems, at times, to be the only life that he has. "Was this all the work a man could find to do?" (104), Herzog asks himself when he finally abandons Sono but only to rush straight into the arms of Madeleine.

What then is to be learned in the female realm? After the breakup of his marriage to Madeleine, Herzog does the rounds of all the women who have witnessed the relationship from its inception. What he uncovers is a web of deceit masquerading under the guise of friendly concern. Tennie, Madeleine's mother, has kind words for Herzog, but she has facilitated her daughter's affair by dragging her granddaughter off to the zoo and leaving her bedroom vacant for Gersbach and Madeleine. Zelda, Madeleine's aunt, is equally two-faced. She has told Herzog lies on Madeleine's behalf, but when Herzog comes to visit she lays on him claims of honesty and friendship. Almost without exception, the women that Herzog knows, even when they are sympathetic to his predicament, cannot resist the opportunity to practice secrecy and intrigue and to gossip.

Gossip, however, is a crucial resource for the subordinated, and like the women of a Muslim harem who assert the value of their own community by critically analyzing the world of men, the women in Herzog's "female realm"—lacking public occupation, beaten down by relationships with cheating, demanding men, and cut off, as almost all of them are, from responsibility for the world's "important affairs"—turn their energies to more intimate forms of communication.

Of course, in the United States, in the second half of the twentieth century, "the female realm" is not exclusively inhabited by females, and the problem for Herzog is that the values and assumptions associated for centuries with the lives of women are now his for the sharing. As an out-of-work professor with an "unemployed consciousness" and a tendency to become involved in erotic entanglements, Herzog is bound to be drawn to those sustaining activities of the hidden private life—sex and gossip. However, gossip, whether in its negative form of distilled malice or its higher Kirkegaardian formulation as "idle talk," fails to satisfy Herzog as a compensation for what he feels is an ineffectual life. Herzog is "bursting with unrecognized needs, imperatives [and] desires for activity," but because he is "too weak" and "unable to struggle with social injustice," he "struggles with women . . . with his 'unhappiness'" instead (208). Herzog has all the sex and talk that he could want, but he wants something more.

Paradoxically, the arch-deceiver in *Herzog*—Madeleine herself—is not really a subject of "the female realm" at all. For, although she indulges in sex and secrecy, they are not the theoretical mainstays of her ideological position. Madeleine, who cheats on Herzog for years with Herzog's best friend, Valentine Gersbach, is an imperious, ambitious young woman who is cold-hearted and manipulative. Madeleine is clearly aligned with those characters in *Herzog*, mostly male, whom Herzog labels "Reality Instructors." These characters, like the lawyer Sandor Himmelstein or the psychoanalyst Dr. Edvig, wish to "punish Herzog with the lessons of the real" (125), to educate him in the harsh, tough ways of the world from which he has supposedly shielded himself. Such shielding, in the terms of Bellow's gender dichotomies, is characteristically "feminine": "He wondered at times whether he didn't belong to a class of people secretly convinced they had an arrangement with fate; in return for docility or ingenuous good will they were to be shielded from the worst brutalities of life. . . . he considered whether he really had inwardly decided years ago to set up a deal—a psychic offer—meekness in exchange for preferential treatment. Such a bargain was feminine . . . childlike" (154).

These "feminine" constituents in Herzog's being are almost more troubling to him, because he is more ambivalent about them, than his confinement to "the female realm." The fate of the intellectual with an "unemployed consciousness" is, after all, culturally dictated; whereas the makeup of Herzog's individual psyche would appear to be something over which he should be able to exert a greater measure of control.

Bellow's delineation of the "feminine" or "female" parts of Herzog's self are, on the surface, traditional and stereotypical. Herzog, who has inherited from his mother a "good heart [and] a gentle spirit" (134), seems also to have inherited her lack of ruthlessness and oversensitivity, both of which render him vulnerable to the Reality Instructors. Through the continuing terms of Bellow's associations we learn that Herzog, governed as he is by "the law of the heart," is bound to those members of society—children, the feebleminded, and most women—who see the world from a different perspective—one that the dominant male culture generally views as immature, idiotic, and overly and irrationally governed by feelings.

The fact that the "law of the heart" (the term is Hegel's although Rousseau's *Je sens mon coeur et je connais les hommes* is also a refrain of Herzog's) is, in both the terms of Herzog's and Bellow's associations, "feminine" is at the base of much of Herzog's ambivalence about himself and about the true nature of the world that he inhabits. Herzog, it seems, both loves and fears the feminine part of himself. The love stems from his faith that the "feminine" elements in his being—his love, feelings, naivete, innocence—permit him to see through the harsh vision of the world offered by the Reality Instructors to an altogether more beneficent and truer reality. The fear derives from the fact that, almost despite himself, Herzog seems to experience a measure of the general American male anxiety that to be a poet, writer, intellectual, or "sensitive person" is actually to be a "woman." In an interview that he gave to *Life* magazine in 1970, Bellow described how writers of his generation "suffer from the persistent American feeling that the intellectual life is somehow not virile. Artists and Professors like clergymen and librarians, are thought to be female. Our populist tradition requires the artist to represent himself as a man of the people and to conceal his real concern with thought."[27]

Herzog seems unsure whether to be characterized as a woman, in the manner described by Bellow, is acceptable or a disaster. Herzog is equally unsure whether the elevation of his "feminine" attributes has rewarded him with additional insight or contributed toward his emasculation—and probably, if Herzog's troubles with Madeleine are anything to go by, it has done both.

Critics have often complained that there are no "real women" in *Herzog,* and although this supposed failure of characterization is taken up in chapter 7, it is important at this stage to distinguish between female characters, what they represent, and what Bellow conceives of as "the feminine." "The feminine" is embodied most powerfully in *Herzog* not in female characters but in the consciousness of the hero, where it resides as a kind of internal woman or internal mother. The wisdom that issues from this feminine wellspring is at the base of Herzog's optimistic affirmations about the world. However, Herzog also remains to some degree permanently discomforted by the notion that a failure to acknowledge the harsh realities of life is concomitant with a failure to be a man.

Plenty of characters take time out to tell Herzog that the reason that he keeps getting screwed is that this is a dog-eat-dog world in which the ruthless triumph and the softies are trampled underfoot. If you allow your feelings to dictate your behavior, you are likely to become the victim of practical realists, people governed partly by malice and hungry for power, individuals who love cruelly to educate the naive in the ways of the world. In *Herzog,* such characters, whether male or female, are "the Real Men," and Herzog, who often lampoons himself in much the same way as the Reality Instructors lampoon him—that is, by describing himself as "childish," "comical," or "softheaded"—is clearly to be excluded from the category. However, Herzog's ironies at his own expense have been designed by Bellow to seduce the reader into sympathizing with his protagonist rather than to confirm the views of Herzog's enemies. What is foregrounded in Herzog's personality is his generosity of being, his brilliance, and his emotional and intellectual superiority over almost all who surround him. Bellow makes sure that Herzog does not come across as the "frail, hopeful lunatic" (106) that Herzog playfully likes to describe himself as.

Herzog, however, remains troubled by the fact that what he is—an unemployed intellectual—and what he has recently experienced—a series of betrayals and humiliations visited on him by Madeleine and her cohorts—have somehow combined to emasculate him. Herzog, in a sense, falls into a trap that the culture has set for him. Male American intellectuals, poets, and novelists have always been dangerously susceptible to the emasculating myths that surround their activities, and in the overtly macho antics of some American writers—such as Norman Mailer's brawling or Frederick Exley's boozing—we witness attempts to counterbalance these myths. Moses Herzog is no exception, for he takes great pleasure in playing the tough guy. His girlfriend Ramona finds this one of the funniest things about him. "It's the way you try to sound rough and reckless though—like a guy from Chicago—that's even more amusing." "Why amusing?" "It's an act. Swagger. It's not really you" (118). Ramona's insight seems to be Bellow's way of reminding us that even Herzog is afflicted with a measure of the self-loathing that he notes with distaste in other intellectuals.

Intellectual life has, then, come to be seen by many of those who live it as unmanly, purposeless, and futile. Herzog, who, to a certain extent, experiences all these feelings, nevertheless feels himself fundamentally grateful to the democratizing civilization that has enabled him to pursue so freely his purposeless activities. Herzog feels that he has "been spared the chief ambiguity that afflicts intellectuals and this is that civilized individuals hate and resent the civilization that makes their lives possible" (304). Why should this be so? In one respect the resentment of the intellectuals is directly related to the peculiarity of their position in society (their essentially "female" position). Too many intelligent people, says Herzog, are "*without influence*" and feel a self-contempt that is reflective of the contempt that is held for them by "*those who hold real political or social power, or think they do*" (161).

But it is not only intellectuals or even "intelligent people" who seem to hate and resent the place that they occupy in contemporary American life. The bitterness and disillusion of the intellectuals is only symptomatic of a larger crisis of consciousness, one that Herzog finds to be affecting virtually everybody. "Consciousness," says Herzog, "when it doesn't clearly understand what to live for, what to die for, can only abuse and ridicule itself" (272). The pressing problem for contemporary men and women is how to fill the vacuum that has been created by our release from painful, necessary, and unavoidable labor and from general physical hardship. The paradox is that we have partly lost our sense of how to live and of what to do with our freedom because the instrument of our liberation—technology—has absorbed so much of value into itself. As Herzog points out "*It is 'good' to electrify a primitive area. . . . Good is easily done by machines of production and transportation*" (164). If we despise the technological civilization that has freed us, on an unprecedented scale, from the fundamental woes and miseries that have accompanied much of daily life throughout history, it must be because technology has also stolen from us that human faculty of which we have been most proud—our moral sense.

From Herzog's perspective we have been freed, finally, on a mass scale, to give ourselves up, like the lucky few citizens of the Greek city-state, to the attainment of "*beauty, nobility, integrity, intensity*" (165), but the liberated individuals of the late twentieth century nevertheless feel themselves terribly obstructed by the nature of mass civilization itself. In this civilization the salience of the individual is constantly being undermined, and any attempt to compete in the area of "doing good" is dwarfed by the enormous but anonymous achievements of science and technology. The results, as Herzog gauges them, are, among the intellectual community, a turn to nihilism and an adoption of what he calls a "wasteland outlook" (75) and, among the community at large, adherence to a general standard of hard-hearted realism. The thinking of the latter group, generated perhaps by its collective unconscious, seems to be something along the lines of, "If the only real good to be done is already being done by benevolent technology, we might as well abandon our quest for a dignified moral life and indulge in some affectless cheating, betraying, and lying."

Although aware of the nature and depth of the problem, Herzog nevertheless opposes both the intellectual's flight into nihilism and the community's apparent suspension of belief in any world except one governed by the corrupt and the phony. Herzog asserts that "*there are moral realities . . . as surely as there are molecular and atomic ones*" (178). By which he means that such values as order, peace, honor, and beauty are not chimerical qualities only to be found harmoniously accruing at the end of a Shakespearean romance (emblems in the external world of achieved spiritual equilibrium for the individual characters) but visionary norms that, if we maintain an allegiance to them, may be made real in our own lives.

As the critic Lionel Trilling pointed out not long after the publication of *Herzog*, we have no trouble with this kind of idea when it emanates, safely distanced, from Shakespeare, but when we hear it from one of our own we tend to get a little perturbed. Saul Bellow's attempt, through the character of Moses Herzog, to assert the claims of these "visionary norms" in the prevailing climate of contemporary literature where they are everywhere rejected and negated is, in fact, so unusual and our surprise so great that we do not know how to respond except with discomfort and embarrassment.[28] To a large degree, contemporary culture has embraced the Reality Instructors' position. When we think of what the world is "really like," we think of the nightly chain of horrors that is the television news, and the politicians whom we tend to assess as having a strong grip on reality are usually those, like Henry Kissinger, whose vision is uncompromisingly pragmatic. Herzog's position is an affront to the sense of reality of both Bellow's readers and Herzog's fellow characters. Herzog does not deny that there is brutality in the world, nor is he indifferent to the wars and genocides of the twentieth century. What disturbs him is the sense of inescapable brutality that has seeped into every area of life—

including the personal realm where he is most involved—so much so that not to act in hard-hearted, "realistic" fashion is now viewed in terms of a failure to fulfill one's proper role as a late twentieth-century person.

But what then are the grounds of Herzog's hopeful assertions about the nature of reality? After all, the experiences that have surrounded the breakup of his marriage to Madeleine have been characterized, almost without exception, by deceit and treachery, and while Herzog has been on his mental rounds reasserting his faith in brotherhood, his fraternity of friends—his lawyer, Sandor Himmelstein; his analyst, Dr. Edvig; his best friend, Valentine Gersbach—have been equally busy, as Herzog points out "giving him the business" (193). Himmelstein passes his lawyer's fees from Herzog onto Madeleine so that she can buy clothes; Edvig becomes fascinated with Herzog's session descriptions of Madeleine, asks to meet her, and then, captivated, turns against his own patient; while Gersbach's long affair with Madeleine is conducted simultaneously to his holding best-friend status in Herzog's life.

There are compelling exceptions among Herzog's friends, relatives, and acquaintances—individuals who are guided by a sense of honor and who act with "gratuitous" kindness. These characters include Lucas Asphalter, Herzog's zoologist friend, who, despite his eccentricity (Asphalter has tried to resuscitate his tubercular, dying monkey Rocco with the kiss of life) embodies a "faithfulness" and "generosity" that Herzog admires; Herzog's brother Will, whose personality develops around an essential "sweet decency"; and the magistrate whom Herzog witnesses behaving with patience and humanity toward the bizarre defendants in his courtroom. But despite the existence of these few good men (the women, as we know, are another story) we cannot assert with any confidence that Herzog's affirmations derive from his immediate experience of life.

In fact, Herzog's repudiation of contemporary nihilism—of the idea, apparently subscribed to by millions, that "truth is true only as it brings down more disgrace and dreariness upon human beings, so that if it shows anything except evil it is illusion, and not truth" (93)—is, quite simply, based on his feelings. Herzog does not want to believe that "*the realm of facts and that of values are . . . eternally separated*" (106). But in order to hold on to his belief he must do two things: trust his feelings and redefine "facts." In these endeavors Herzog comes up against both internal and external opposition. "Feelings," as I have already suggested, and this is where the internal opposition comes in, are "female" and "childish" in terms of both Herzog's and Bellow's associations. "Facts," by contrast, are "male" and "adult." As Adrienne Rich notes in her book *On Lies, Secrets and Silence,* "Men have been expected to tell the truth about facts, not about feelings. They have not been expected to talk about feelings at all."[29] But for Herzog, almost the only facts worth talking about are those that can be ascertained and confirmed through feeling. Predictably, the external opposition in this area is powerful.

Herzog's most vocal antagonist is his Chicago lawyer, Sandor Himmelstein. A bullying, manipulative individual with an uncontrollable propensity to smash plates in his kitchen when he gets excited, Himmelstein is a ridiculous figure but one who commands our attention because he also happens to be the novel's liveliest exponent of tough-minded realism. Herzog wants Himmelstein to sue on his behalf for custody of his daughter, Junie, but Sandor has other ideas. Indeed, his most powerful desire is to cut "the dead weight of deception from Herzog's soul" (84). The facts are ugly, Moses may be in the right, but the courts will go for Madeleine nevertheless. "They'll look at Madeleine, blooming and lovely, then you, haggard and gray-haired, and bam! there goes your custody suit. That's the jury system. Dumber than cave men, those bastards—I know this isn't easy for you to hear but I better say it. Guys at our time of life must face facts" (83). Herzog does not wholly reject Sandor's jaundiced view of the American legal system but nevertheless has an altogether different idea of what constitutes a fact:

> "Do you know what a mass man is Himmelstein? . . . A man of the crowd. The soul of the mob. Cutting everybody down to size?"
>
> "What soul of the mob! Don't get highfalutin. I'm talking facts, not shit."
>
> "And you think a fact is what's nasty."

> "Facts *are* nasty."
> "You think they're true because they're nasty." (86).

For Himmelstein, as for all the Reality Instructors and everyone else who has jumped on the fashionable contemporary philosophical bandwagon ("Everybody was in on the act. . . The very Himmelsteins, who had never even read a book of metaphysics, were touting the void" [93]), "facts," "nasty," and "truth" are synonyms. Herzog wants to believe otherwise, he at least wants to assert a meliorist position. "*Mild or moderate truthfulness*" is what Herzog is after, but, as he notes, such unextravagant yearning "*seems to have no pull at all*" (316).

Whose version of reality does the novel as a whole endorse? The Reality Instructors' or Herzog's? Late in the novel Herzog seems to acknowledge that there has been extremism on both sides. "I shouldn't look down on old Sandor for being so tough. This is his personal, brutal version of the popular outlook, the American way of life. And what has my way been? I love little pussy, her coat is so warm, and if I don't hurt her she'll do me no harm, which represents the childish side of the same creed, from which men are wickedly awakened, and then become snarling realists" (291). The battle lines here between Himmelstein and Herzog seem to be drawn along philosophical lines that invite labeling as Realist and Romantic. Indeed, throughout the novel, Herzog toys with a Romantic perspective that is easily associated with all things private, interior, and female. The Romantic view, among other perspectives, elevates subjectivity, foregrounds feelings, and asserts the claims of the individual in the face of alien and crushing necessity. Herzog, however, despite the fact that he is drawn to Romanticism, is also a skeptic. Herzog's academic work, before he abandoned it, was directed toward exposing flaws in Romantic philosophy, "overturning the last of the Romantic errors about the uniqueness of the Self" (39), and revealing the relationship between Romantic thought and totalitarianism. Herzog is equally skeptical of those strains of Romanticism that filtered into contemporary life and seem to have infected a large number of individuals with the desire to glorify sickness and poverty and uncover genius in mental illness. Herzog has little or not time for characters, like his childhood friend Nachman, who traffic in such ideas.

Herzog is neither a holder of exclusively Romantic views nor the dreamy naif that he likes to paint himself as. When he tells us that unlike his brothers (both tough businessmen, the elder of whom is ruthless enough to be labeled "a true disciple of Thomas Hobbes" [78]) he is a specialist "in spiritual self-awareness; or emotionalism; or ideas; or nonsense" (307), the description concurs with the personality of Herzog that we extrapolate from the novel only if we drop the undermining "nonsense."

Bellow's Herzog, as opposed to Herzog's Herzog, is a Romantic/Realist, self-aware, emotional, and full of ideas but *not* self-indulgent, lachrymose, and unreachably abstruse. In similar fashion, the representatives of Realism turn out to be somewhat afflicted with the worst strains of Romanticism. The "brutality" of Himmelstein and Gersbach is, as Herzog points out, always accompanied by a flabby moral sentimentalism. What is more, as the novel makes quite clear, the "brutality" of these characters turns out in the end to be not quite so brutal after all. As Herzog begins to get over Madeleine and his cuckold's venom starts to dissipate, he begins to regard the Reality Instructors less as malevolent beings than as comedic figures; objects not of scorn but of wry sympathy. Even the prime actors in Herzog's drama, Madeleine and Gersbach, are eventually released by Herzog into the stream of common humanity where he can shake his head and laugh at them. The novel, that begins by apparently offering the reader a choice between endorsing quite distinct views of the world (Romantic or Real; innocent or experienced; soft-hearted or hard-hearted) ends by shoring up a melioristic position, one that has been intellectually established by Herzog but is, despite initial appearances to the contrary, enacted by the majority of the characters in the text.

V

Ideas

Herzog is a novel of ideas, a novel about people who have ideas, and a novel that seeks to debunk pervasive purveyors of ideas and explanations. Herzog's ideas and those of the other characters and figures in the novel are related at almost every point to Herzog's own troubled life. What may appear at first to be Herzog's esoteric wrestling with the maxims, thoughts, and speculations of dead philosophers whose work is applicable to a vanished world soon reveals itself as a struggle not only with ideas that still hold their relevance and importance today but also with individuals who, crossing boundaries of space and time, seem to embody fully or partially one or more of the stages in the history of ideas that is Herzog's playing field. Thus, for example, modernist crisis ethics can be found in Sandor Himmelstein, a streak of Calvinism in Dr. Edvig, extreme Romanticism in Nachman and George Hoberly, and so on.

In each period and with each discipline that Herzog engages he seems able to team up with at least one major thinker and oppose another: in this way Herzog can take on Hobbes with the aid of Spinoza in the seventeenth century; Rousseau with the aid of Blake in the eighteenth; Marx with Tolstoy in the nineteenth; and Freud with some metaphysical speculations of his own in the twentieth. Concurrent to Herzog's intellectual battles are analogous conflicts with individuals, present in his own life, who are the distortive epigones of their great philosophical precursors. When Herzog argues with Hobbes, he is also setting himself against the worldview of his hard-hearted businessman brother, Shura; when he criticizes Rousseau's "cult of the ego," he is simultaneously finding fault with Valentine Gersbach; when he contradicts Freud, it is also a strike against his analyst, Dr. Edvig. Herzog's personal relations thus reflect and refract his internal ideological battles.

Many first-time readers of *Herzog* are likely to be put off by the range of Herzog's erudition and the breadth of his references. After all, Herzog's field is history, most particularly the philosophy of history and political and moral philosophy, and although we are not given any excerpts from his books to read, we do witness him in imaginary correspondence, or mental dialogue, with, among others, Montaigne, Pascal, Spinoza, Rousseau, Kant, Fichte, Nietzsche, Hulme, Heidegger, and Spengler. Does one need to be as learned as Herzog in order fully to understand what is going on in this novel? It probably helps, but it can safely be assumed that very few Bellow readers are as well read in philosophy as either Herzog or Bellow, and it seems unlikely that Bellow intended to limit his reading audience to those who shared Herzog's area of specialization.

Herzog's relation to philosophical speculation in general is, in any case, outlined quite clearly early in the novel, and we soon gather that Herzog is skeptical of much modern thought.

> *Very tired of the modern form of historicism which sees in this civilization the defeat of the best hopes of Western religion and thought, what Heidegger calls the second Fall of Man into the quotidian or ordinary. No philosopher knows what the ordinary is, has not fallen into it deeply enough.* (106)

For Herzog, "the ordinary" must be the testing ground of all ideas, and Herzog likes to puncture ideas that are appealing in the abstract, like the above thought of Heidegger's, by rendering their seductive metaphors literal. "*Dear Doktor Professor Heidegger,*" he writes, "*I should like to know what you mean by the expression 'the fall into the quotidian.' When did this fall occur? Where were we standing when it happened*" (49).

Herzog is a thinker who is suspicious of thinkers. There are two main reasons for this. First, the content of much contemporary thought, coming out of German existentialism (which itself Herzog sees as deriving from a Christian, primarily Protestant, view of history), regards "the present moment always as some crisis, some fall from classic greatness, some corruption or evil to be saved from." Herzog regards this as a niggardly view, "foolish dreariness," a projection onto history of the private fantasies of intellectuals. For Herzog it is of prime importance that we "*get it out of our heads that this is a doomed time*" (316). If we don't we will end up believing the stories that we like to scare ourselves with and, in some terminally irresponsible manner, act in ways that will ensure the advent of the doom that we prophesy. Of those who subscribe to current nihilistic thought fads Herzog would like to ask,

> *Are all the traditions used up, the beliefs done for. . . . Is this the full crisis of dissolution? Has the filthy moment come when moral feeling dies, conscience disintegrates, and respect for liberty, law, public decency, all the rest, collapses in cowardice, decadence, blood? Old Proudhon's visions of darkness and evil can't be passed over. But we mustn't forget how quickly the visions of genius become the canned goods of the intellectuals. The canned sauerkraut of Spengler's "Prussian Socialism," the commonplaces of the Wasteland outlook, the cheap mental stimulants of alienation, the cant and rant of pipsqueaks about Inauthenticity and Forlornness. I can't accept this. . . . We are talking about the whole life of mankind. The subject is too great, too deep for such weakness, cowardice.* (74–75)

It is time, Herzog argues in his never-ending stream of mental letters, that we stopped talking about human nature being this or that or the other thing. Total explanations are a delusion, "human life" says Herzog "is far subtler than any of its models" (271).

Second, Herzog distrusts a great deal of philosophy because it has not done him any good. Here he is an educated, possibly overeducated, man who has at his fingertips the thoughts and theories of the great thinkers of Western culture, and yet he cannot manage the conduct of his daily life except in the most haphazard and confused way.

In addition to being skeptical of philosophies of total explanation, Herzog is even suspicious of many of his own ideas, for he recognizes that they are not the product of clear intellectual rigor but an ideational spillage from his emotional problems.

Herzog's marital crisis has "heightened his perceptions" (278), but he is chary of the insights that these heightened perceptions have spawned. Conceiving of himself as "an industry that manufactures personal history" (3), Herzog is an essentially autonomous institution imaginatively geared up by his personal crises and sustained by the wildly complex figurations that his sexual sublimations throw up. Herzog, in fact, is a sophisticated alchemist of personal crisis: his narrative turns the dross of a troubled personal life into an elevated discussion of all those philosophers and all their *isms.*

Herzog's performance is quite dazzling; thoughts, associations, grand and petty ideas, run, leap, pound, and tingle through his brain with astonishing rapidity, but as he himself acknowledges, his ideas are the flotsam and jetsam of a troubled mind—superfluities, distractions. Herzog's ultimate goal seems to be the achievement of a kind of transcendental peace.

Unlike the thinkers, writers, and politicians toward whom he is antagonistic, Herzog does not want to synthesize his thought into something that offers the illusion of all-embracing wholeness. Herzog, rather, yearns to still the babble of tongues inside him, to rid his mind of clutter, and to exorcise the ghosts of his disastrous marriage to Madeleine. Herzog's ideas, at their current rarified level and intriguing and worthy as they may be, would not exist were it not for the emotional crisis that he has found himself in. The emotional crisis is one that Herzog would like to end, and he is quite willing to sacrifice his brilliant insights, ideas, and perceptions if it means that he will be able to come to terms with Madeleine and achieve some inner and outer peace. For Herzog, ideas are not hierarchically superior to peace of mind. They are a kind of by-product on the route to achieving it.

Despite the fact that, ultimately, the content of Herzog's ideas is not important to Herzog, it is important to his readers. Herzog's thoughts are, of course, "private," and Herzog rightly feels that he has, in Whitman's phrase, "*[e]scaped from the life that exhibits itself*" (324). In fact, he is scornful of those (like his earlier self) who wish to rise up before their fellow man and say, "*I am here to witness. I am come to be your exemplar*" (324). The desire to foist one's opinions, views, ideas, and philosophies on others, is, from one of Herzog's current perspectives, simply the result of an overflow of narcissism. Despite Herzog's reservations, however, Bellow seems to think enough of Herzog's private ideas and thoughts to want to make them public: although Herzog's narrative is not addressed directly to the reader (his first-person reflections and meditations are filtered through a third-person narrative), Bellow's is.

Herzog's philosophical perspective is revealed to us through his mental letters and thoughts, which, although they are scattered throughout the text and appear disconnected, accumulate by the end of the novel into a solid ideational position. To reduce Herzog's responses to their simplest level, we might say that he is not pleased with existentialism, the absurd, and other aspects of modernist ideology. He is equally put off by the utopianism of Marxists and contemporary apocalypse-mongering, which Herzog sees as an outgrowth of dangerous nineteenth-century Romantic dreams. Herzog is ambivalent about Romanticism and suspicious of Freudianism. On the plus side, Herzog is serious about transcendence, the soul, the individual, community, brotherhood, the heart, the value of reason, the metaphysical, and a kind of idiosyncratic cultural Jewishness—but one that is certainly not grounded in religious observance.

Herzog's argument with existentialism and its proponents (Sartre is always a favorite Bellow target) is, as we have already seen, forcefully in evidence in *Herzog*. Herzog wishes to challenge and displace the existential or Christian view of history. He is sick of those who "tout the Void as if it were so much saleable real estate" (93), but he is also disturbed by the existential denial of essence (the basic tenet of existential philosophy being that existence precedes essence—Herzog unabashedly believes in the soul) and by its deification of death, something that Herzog lays at the doorstep of German existentialism and most particularly the philosophy of Martin Heidegger. "But what is the philosophy of this generation?" Herzog asks himself. "Not God is dead, that point was passed long ago. Perhaps it should be stated Death is God. This generation thinks—and this is its thought of thoughts—that nothing faithful, vulnerable, fragile can be durable or have any true power. Death waits for these things as a cement floor waits for a dropping light bulb" (290). Herzog does not attempt to put death aside—indeed, he expends much thought on the subject—but he sees his own excessive morbidity as a symptom of his current disorder. Herzog's true perspective on death is a combination of Blake's vitalist instruction to "Drive your cart and your plow over the bones of the dead" and his slightly less radical personal credo "perpetual thought of death was a sin" (33).

The dangers and foolishness of death obsession are clarified toward the end of *Herzog* when Herzog pays a short visit to his old friend Lucas Asphalter. Asphalter, a zoologist, has been in a terrible state mourning the death of his favorite monkey. In order to get himself out of his depression Asphalter has consulted a quirky analyst, Tina Zokoly, whose therapeutic process demands that patients confront death by imagining themselves already in their coffins. Tina Zokoly is clearly a domesticated Heideggerian ("'Face death. That's Heidegger'" [207], says Herzog as Asphalter tells him the story), and she is satirized in the novel in much the same way as Heidegger when the "abstract" imaginings that she demands of Asphalter are revealed crashing on the rocks of the zoologist's concrete memories. As Asphalter lies in his imaginary coffin and tries to come up with thoughts on his own death, all that enters his mind are comic images. First, Asphalter conjures his Aunt Rae being rescued from a fire when he was a little boy: he remembers watching a fireman come down the ladder that has been raised outside his house, the fireman has Aunt Rae over his shoulder and he is "red in the face from the weight and strain," but even more powerfully Asphalter recalls Aunt Rae's huge buttocks descending toward him, a small boy watching from the ground, "the tremendous rear part, the huge cheeks, so pale and helpless" (270). Asphalter's second childhood memory is of witnessing street softball games played by burlesque dancers in full costume. The young women, performers in a sleazy theater next door to young Asphalter's home, used to come out between turns to have some fun on an empty lot that Asphalter could see from his bedroom window. For Herzog, and for Bellow too, here is the life—rich, warm, perhaps comic, but authentic and meaningful nonetheless—that asserts itself against the theories of fear and anguish that contemporary thinkers and their nonsensical epigones like Tina Zokoly would impose on us.

Asphalter's visions also have something to say to those who have bought into T. S. Eliot's bleak vision of twentieth-century life as a contemporary wasteland; individuals who accept and endorse the spare, dry concept of humanity that Eliot and his anti-Romantic precursor, the philosopher T. E. Hulme, have promoted. The juiciness of Asphalter's memories—the Felliniesque "burlesque broads . . . all powdered and rouged . . . their hair done up, their tits heaving as they pitched and batted and ran the bases" (271), and the "fat-assed old auntie saved from death" (270)—are profoundly antithetical to the sterility and impotence that, in Herzog's opinion, Hulme, Eliot, and their followers made a religion out of.

Asphalter's behavior in therapy also demonstrates human nature resisting contours of arrest. In this case, Asphalter is evading Tina Zokoly's morbid definitions, but for Herzog his reactions also remind us of the unclassifiable qualities of human nature itself. "*Man has a nature, but what is it?*" says Herzog. "*Those who have confidently described it, Hobbes, Freud, et cetera, by telling us what we are 'intrinsically,' are not our greatest benefactors. This is true also for Rousseau. . . . perhaps a moratorium on definitions of human nature is now best*" (129).

Hobbes, Rousseau, Freud, and others who have "confidently described" human nature are not our greatest benefactors because, if we accept their definitions, we accept that our fate is determined. Moreover, the views of these thinkers too often can be seen to advance politically dangerous philosophies or nihilism.

For Hobbes, life, in his famous phrase, is "nasty, brutish and short," and human beings are governed by unruly passions that, were they not kept in check by the power of the state, would lead them into anarchy. There are plenty of Hobbesians in *Herzog* (including Herzog's own brother, Shura), individuals who respond to "nasty, brutish and short" as if it were a prescription for behavior. Against the Hobbesian vision Herzog would set that of Spinoza, who, writing, like Hobbes, in the seventeenth century, was nevertheless forward looking enough to view reason, freedom, and happiness as contingent human pursuits. Spinoza too, as Herzog's sporadic references to him indicate, remained confident enough in the human potential for virtue to envisage the state not merely as a bulwark against human disasters but as a force to promote positive human goodness.

Herzog's relationship to Rousseau and to Romanticism in general is more complex. As I have noted, the Romantic emphasis on the mantic properties of the heart is important to Herzog and he concurs when Rousseau says "*Je sens mon coeur et je connais les hommes*" (340). In fact, Herzog's adherence to the values of the heart seems to have its derivation even earlier in his reading of Pascal. Pascal, with his rather labored attempts to "prove" Christianity through biblical criticism, is not a philosopher whom one would think would have much appeal to Herzog. However, Pascal is also, like Montaigne, one of the few thinkers that Herzog unreservedly admires because he does not evade the complexity and singularity of situations by blanketing them in monolithic theory. In addition, Pascal's *Pensee* 110 (*Le coeur a ses raisons que la raison ne connait pas*) could almost be read as a summary of Herzog's own philosophy—in the extent to which that philosophy is extrapolatable.

> We know the truth not only through our reason but also through our heart. It is through the latter that we know first principles, and

> reason, which has nothing to do with it, tries in vain to refute them. . . . We know that we are not dreaming, but, however unable we may be to prove it rationally, our inability proves nothing but the weakness of our reason, and not the uncertainty of all our knowledge. . . . For knowledge of first principles . . . is as solid as any derived through reason, and it is on such knowledge . . . coming from the heart and instinct, that reason has to depend and base all its argument.[30]

If the prompting of the heart is valuable to Herzog, so too is the quiddity of the self. Unfortunately, Romantic emphasis on the self can become obsessive. Rousseau is to be held responsible for the emergence of the cult of ego and therefore, in Herzog's opinion, can also be charged with creating the philosophical climate that, in the very long run, produced a bloated, sloppy, puffed up, sentimental soul like Valentine Gersbach. Gersbach is in love with his own personality, and Herzog is terribly weary of those who flaunt themselves under the expressive banner of "being themselves." What is important for Gersbach is the intensity of an experience, not its content. Whether he is talking about Martin Buber or lecturing Herzog on the conduct of his marriage, or recalling a genuine tragedy—his childhood loss of his leg in a railroad accident—the same willed tears (what Milan Kundera calls the "second tear" or "meta-tear" that is the sign of pure kitsch)[31] will well up in his eyes. The fact that Gersbach is a complete hypocrite—his advice to Herzog on how to save his marriage is given while he is sleeping with Madeleine—and a phony—his contrived intellectuality is a poor imitation of Herzog's own, "a parody of the intellectual's desire for higher meaning, depth, quality" (60)—does not prevent him, in his own eyes and in the eyes of others, from indulging and promoting his glorious self.

Despite the obvious deficiencies of a Gersbach or Madeleine herself, when it comes to issues of the self, Herzog finds himself in something of a quandary. Although he rejects wholeheartedly the Romantic overinflation of the self—even to the point of sympathizing with T. E. Hulme's attack on the Romantics for their belief in human perfectibility—for Herzog man *may* have created God but that does not mean that he is God. The individual nevertheless remains the center of value for Herzog.

Herzog recognizes that the Romantic spirit has guarded what Herzog calls "*the 'inspired condition'*" and thus preserved "*the poetic, philosophical, and religious teachings, the teachings and records of transcendence and the most generous ideas of mankind, during the greatest and most rapid of transformations, the most accelerated phase of the modern scientific and technical transformation*" (165). However, once again, Herzog turns out to be only half-hearted in his Romantic allegiance. Romantic individuals (and Herzog finds that there is "*a mass of them*" [165] still knocking around in the twentieth century) believe that the only way to attain "the inspired condition" in which one is able "*to know truth, to be free, to love another, to consummate existence, to abide with death in the clarity of consciousness*" (165) is to travel the route of excess via drugs, the polymorphous sexual perversity that Herzog calls "the religion of civilized people" (24), or some gratuitous, "philosophical" criminal act (when Bellow has Herzog take a dig at those who pursue the "*inspired condition . . . in the negative . . . in literature*" [164], he clearly has in mind novels in which Romanticism and existentialism overlap and that feature protagonists like Camus's Meursault, descendant of Dostoyevski's Raskolnikov and precursor of Norman Mailer's Stephen Rojack). Herzog does not want to believe that narcotics, sexual excess, and motiveless murder transport one to truth more efficiently and rapidly than harmless old "*decency . . . honor or . . . courage*" (164). As Herzog likes to point out, to behave with decency to another human being is also "gratuitous." Fortunately for Herzog he does not have to deal personally with the contemporary excessive types that he witnesses American culture nurturing—Dionysian students strung out on sex and drugs will be the unworthy antagonists of Bellow's next hero, Artur Sammler—but in the emotional and intellectual dilettantism of some of his adversaries, particularly Madeleine and Gersbach, Herzog thinks that he sees a disdain for basic human values and a resolve to get at the truth via less than salutary means.

If the legacy of Romantic individualism has been damaging, the political fallout from certain Romantic ideas, particularly those concerned with apocalypse, has been much more dangerous. An impatience for apocalypse seems to have taken hold among the general population of North America. Herzog is all too well aware of the terrible disasters that have sprung from revolutionary idealism—Rousseau's social contract, with its elevation of the *volonté genérale* of the people spawned Robespierre's terror: Herzog, we are told "took seriously Heinrich Heine's belief that the words of Rousseau had turned into the bloody machine of Robespierre, that Kant and Fichte were deadlier than armies" (119). Marx's utopian visions of the state withering away were transformed by Lenin and Stalin into the prisons of the Gulag and engineered famines; and in our own time, the idea of turning everything upside down and starting anew is perilous in the extreme as our weapons virtually ensure that there will be no "anew."

The yearning for a cleansing apocalypse derives from the notion that civilization has declined to some terminal point from which it can be retrieved only through radically destructive but simultaneously regenerative action. Although the need for social revolution in the democratic United States hardly seems as pressing as it was in prerevolutionary France or Russia, Herzog sees a far more insidious residual yearning for the end, almost a death instinct, at work in the hearts and minds of some of the country's most solid citizens. It is not only loony Pentagon generals or government scientists who are playing apocalypse (Herzog is "*deeply concerned with the social and ethical reasoning of scientists*," and he warns that some of the people most "*greatly respected in their generation often turn out to be dangerous lunatics*" [49], but even a lawyer like Sandor Himmelstein, picking up on the zeitgeist, is "touting the Void as if it were so much saleable real estate" (93).

Herzog is wary of both crisis-mongers and utopians (two sides of the same coin, really), who offer an idyll to compare with the world as it is. To those whose view of the world is indefatigably bleak Herzog acknowledges that the twentieth century has indeed witnessed humankind living through its darkest times, but the defeat of Hitler and his demonic nihilism and even the economic rejuvenation of Germany (notwithstanding the wry irony with which Herzog views it) are signs of human resilience and political vitality.

Some critics of *Herzog* have viewed both Herzog's and Bellow's political positions as feeble endorsements of the status quo, but Herzog is far from opposed to all kinds of change. In fact, he is quite as repulsed by the blight of American inner cities as his favorite poet, William Blake, was by eighteenth-century London.

Blake is an important figure for Herzog and a fruitful source of relevant quotation. Herzog likes to draw proverbs from "The Marriage of Heaven and Hell" ("Opposition is true friendship" [86], cites the powerfully opposed Herzog) in order to summarize or comment purposefully on his predicament. Moreover, Blake's *Songs of Innocence and Experience*, which, within a single Romantic sensibility, allot equal weight to the naive or childish and the mature workings of a social conscience, are obviously appealing poems for Herzog. As we have seen, Herzog regards the "naive" and "childish" parts of himself as valuable sources of insight that improve rather than impair the accuracy of his vision of the world around him: a vision that does not shirk from social horror.

At times, Herzog seems to be updating Blake's visions of London to contemporary Manhattan. When Herzog visits a Manhattan courthouse, he sees human cruelty and hopelessness on a grand scale, and when he is on the streets of the city, he finds that the Upper West Side can offer visions quite as effecting as Blake's London. In the bizarre crowd that Herzog witnesses traipsing over the broad sidewalk on Upper Broadway, he sees "strong marks of decay" and "signs in almost every passing face of a deeper comment or interpretation of destiny—eyes that held metaphysical statements" (179). What Herzog sees in the faces of the pedestrians does not correspond precisely to Blake's "Marks of weakness, marks of woe," but the "transvestite homosexuals painted with great originality, the wigged women, the lesbians" (179) are, in the prophetic nature of what they communicate, clearly the uptown public's descendants of Blake's "youthful Harlots."

What Herzog's crowd signifies is not a decline into decadence but a yearning for authenticity. Herzog does not tell us as directly as Blake in "London" what he reads in the faces that surround him, but he notes the theatrical, performance-oriented nature of the Broadway crowd, and we can surmise that, like Herzog's desperate night-school students, the crowd is formed of people who are "dying . . . for lack of something real to carry home when day is done." Hence, the extravagant self-parody of the crowd's constituents.

It is Blake the visionary and prophet with whom Herzog is most in sympathy, for Herzog too is something of a voice in the wilderness speaking truths that no one wants to hear. Of course, contemporary Herzog with his heightened self-consciousness and ironic self-awareness does not entertain any notions of achieving a life in the twentieth century that is parallel to Blake's in the eighteenth. Herzog has even given up, as he tells Aunt Zelda, on his fantasies of presenting "a new angle on the human condition" (39). Nevertheless, the plans that Herzog did have in mind for shifting human consciousness, however slightly, are instructive.

In his study, unwritten and unpublished, Herzog intended "to show how life could be lived by renewing universal connections; overturning the last of the Romantic errors about the uniqueness of the Self; revising the old Western, Faustian ideology the social meaning of Nothingness" (39). The closest that Herzog gets in the novel to clarifying his intentions comes when he tells Lucas Asphalter, "I really believe that brotherhood is what makes a man human. If I owe God a human life, this is where I fall down. 'Man liveth not by Self alone but in his brother's face. . . . Each shall behold the Eternal Father and love and joy abound'" (272). Herzog's quotation is again from Blake (*The Four Zoas*), and it is through Blake that Herzog asserts his faith in the value of and need for community.

Although Herzog may use Blake to assert the value of community, the community that Herzog himself inhabits seems a long way from ideal. In a way, this is partly a necessary function of Bellow's modes of characterization. Herzog's antagonists embody ideas that Bellow, along with Herzog, would like to discredit, and so they are painted by Bellow in rather broad strokes. Many of Herzog's adversaries are physically disabled, and Bellow rather cruelly exploits the handicaps that he has given them as a means of negative characterization (Sandor Himmelstein has a hunchback and Valentine Gersbach a wooden leg) or unappealing (Edgar Shapiro sweats inordinately, while Madeleine is a purveyor of unpleasant odors "so proud but not well-wiped") (299). Because these characterizations are filtered through Herzog's consciousness rather than given the authority of an extradiegetal narrator, they can be read as the unreliably hostile descriptions of an angry man. Bellow offers no alternative to Herzog's perspective (we do not learn from Madeleine's *thoughts* what she thinks of Herzog), and Herzog's vision is more or less endorsed by the behavior and dialogue of the other characters in the text, however, so we have little choice but to accept Herzog's descriptions as accurate.

The character who is perhaps undercut most powerfully in the novel is Herzog's and Madeleine's psychoanalyst, Dr. Edvig, and this is as it should be given the importance of Herzog's struggle and engagement with Freudian ideas. Edvig's physical appearance is recognizably parodic; he has a neatly trimmed beard and perfectly shined round glasses—he is supposed to see clearly but doesn't. Edvig's hypocrisy and lack of psychological insight are mercilessly revealed in the text. Edvig alone, among Herzog's opponents, remains unforgiven by Herzog. Herzog's last letter to him begins "*My dear sage and imbecilic Edvig*" (313), and although we can perhaps detect a note of affection here, it is a mute one compared to Herzog's rapturous, Shakespearean release of Madeleine and Gersbach: "*Dear Madeleine—You are a terrific one, you are! Bless you! What a creature! . . . And you, Gersbach, you're welcome to Madeleine. Enjoy her—rejoice in her*" (318).

Bellow felt the need to take issue with Freud for a long time. His play, *The Last Analysis*, is a full-length parody of the analytical process, and his central characters have resisted one aspect or another of Freud's ideas since *The Adventures of Augie March* (1953). The basis of Bellow's argument with Freud is spelt out in two interviews that Bellow gave in the late seventies. Bellow makes it quite clear that what he objects to is seeing the unconscious as a form of determinism. In the first interview Bellow asks, "What is the unconscious after all? The unconscious is anything human beings don't know. . . . Is it possible that what we don't know has a metaphysical character and not a Freudian, natural character? I think that the unconscious is a concept that begs the question and simply returns us to our ignorance with an arrogant attitude of confidence, and this is why I'm against it."[32]

Two years later Bellow had this to add: "Do you believe the psychoanalytic explanation of your deeper motives? Or do you simply say, 'These are my deeper motives, I don't care what psychoanalysis has to say about them.' . . . What a woman does for her children, what a man does for his family, what people most tenaciously cling to, these things are not adequately explained by Oedipus complexes, libidos."[33] The idea that the individual can be pegged, boxed-in, fully known, and surrounded by a theory—and a theory that finds the root of adult human behavior in the life of the infant or child and presupposes that we can never know, as adults, what it is that truly moves us—is clearly unacceptable to Bellow and Herzog both. Even though Bellow's modes of characterization and Herzog's appraisals of his fellow characters are sometimes couched in psychological terms (Herzog describes Gersbach as a "psychopath" and Madeleine as "paranoid"), Bellow's answers to what is "unknown" about the human personality are to be located in the metaphysical (where no final answers may be found), whereas Herzog's affirmations of the soul and his search for transcendent peace are clearly signs that he shares his creator's metaphysical leanings.

Bellow and Herzog may resist the "all embracing" aspect of Freud's theories, but this does not mean that they reject every word that Freud has written. Herzog likes to play with the vocabulary of psychoanalysis to summarize his own character; he is "narcissistic" and "masochistic," and he accepts Dr. Edvig's characterization of him as a "reactive depressive." At the end of the novel Herzog describes his release from Madeleine in psychoanalytic terms that he has derived from Freud's paper "Mourning and Melancholia." But more important than the squibs of insight that Herzog takes from Freud is the way in which he sometimes seems to act in accordance with, rather than in opposition to, Freud's sense of what it means to be a civilized person, a person paying a heavy price for his or her civilized behavior.

The invisible text behind *Herzog* is Freud's *Civilization and Its Discontents*. In this late, bleak book of Freud's the civilized world is described as a place where human beings are painfully and inevitably caught between their values on the one hand and their desires on the other. In *Herzog*, Freud's ideas are recapitulated in a fascinating way, as the rewards of civilization—law, order, civilized behavior—are shown to be won at the expense of great individual frustration. Indeed, at times it almost seems as if the psychology of Moses Herzog has derived directly from Freud's assertion that civilized man has sacrificed much that would make him happy—including the acting out of his sexual and aggressive impulses—for the sake of security and protection. Our assessment and understanding of Herzog's problems can be enhanced if we approach him, in some aspects of his being and *pace* Bellow, as a "living" example of Freud's theories. Herzog, for the most part, lives a fairly comfortable, fairly normal life: he is neither destitute, nor suffering excessively from disease, nor intolerably lonely, nor even overwhelmingly heartbroken. Nevertheless, he displays a frustration and sometimes an anger that without recourse to some notion of suffering as the human condition seems almost ineffable.

The bouts of misery and confusion that Herzog experiences after the breakup of his marriage are quite clearly identified, by him, as stemming from his necessary repression of his deepest yearnings for revenge—necessary because Herzog quite simply does not want to go to jail and because he believes, although it is painful for him to do so, that it is a good thing that the civilized forces of "social organization" (220) exist to keep him in check. Herzog has to satisfy himself with thought violence. He knows that a mental murder a day keeps the psychoanalyst away, but enjoying wild fantasies of what he would like to do to Gersbach and Madeleine—"What if he had knocked her down, clutched her hair, dragged her screaming and fighting around the room, flogged her until her buttocks bled. What if he had! He should have torn her clothes, ripped off her necklace, brought his fists down on her head." (10)—is not quite enough to prevent the repression of action from "coming back as stinging poison" (232).

Where Freud and Bellow diverge, however, is in the conclusions that they draw from their observations of the human condition. For Freud, "unhappiness" is a given—the purpose of psychoanalysis, in his famous dictum, being to move individuals "from neurotic misery to common unhappiness." For Bellow, and Herzog is an exemplary character in this respect, the unhappiness brought on by repression is sporadic and not a permanent state of being. Herzog is able not only to detach himself from his insights into his own misery but also to transcend them. He does not "deal with" his problems by confronting Madeleine and Gersbach and talking things over with them, nor does he attempt to solve his problems on the analyst's couch. Instead, Herzog tends to be brought out of his anger, or unhappy state, by sudden, sometimes intangible, intimations of goodness and grace.

A case in point, and indeed, the turning point of the novel, arises when, after a horrifying experience in a New York courtroom where he has witnessed the trial of two child murderers, Herzog rushes off to Chicago with the avowed intention of killing Madeleine and Gersbach. The defendants in the trial, two brutal, indifferent, pathetic individuals, get tangled up in Herzog's mind with Madeleine and Gersbach, and their crime, which horrifies Herzog, suddenly becomes indistinguishable from the "crime" that Madeleine and Gersbach have committed: Herzog has heard through a third party that the two lovers have locked his daughter Junie in a car outside their house in order that they might get on with a lover's tiff in peace. Herzog goes as far as to pick up an old handgun from the home of his late father, load it with two bullets, and arrive, gun in hand, outside the house where Madeleine and Gersbach are living. But at the house (Herzog's old domicile) everything changes. Gersbach and Mady are not, after all, child murderers; they may have cultivated distasteful personalities, but their essential humanity is intact. This revelation comes to Herzog as he looks through the bathroom window of his old house and sees Gersbach tenderly bathing his daughter Junie.

> There were two bullets in the chamber. . . . But they would stay there. Herzog clearly recognized that. Very softly he stepped down

> from his perch. . . . He edged through the gate into the alley. Firing this pistol was nothing but a thought. (257)

From the moment that Herzog recognizes the actuality of Gersbach and transforms him in his imagination from "a poisonous individual" to a "tender buffoon" (258), he is on the right path to inner peace.

Soon after the incident at his own house Herzog begins to feel, mysteriously, that his "state of simple, free intense realization" (265) is coming to an end. He has time, however, for one last major insight, and it is metaphysical in nature.

> The necessary premise is that a man is somehow more than his "characteristics," all the emotions, strivings, tastes, and constructions which it pleases him to call "My life." We have ground to hope that a Life is something more than such a cloud of particles, mere facticity. Go through what is comprehensible and you conclude that only the incomprehensible gives any light. . . . It all seemed to him exceptionally clear. What made it clear? Something at the very end of the line. Was that thing death? But death was not the incomprehensible accepted by his heart. No, far from it. (266)

That the "unknown" renders us more than we can possibly appear to be and that the "unknown" is a transcendental soul rather than a natural unconscious seems clear. Freud could probably find an explanation for Herzog's unwillingness to shoot Madeleine and Gersbach or the sudden fleeting affection that Herzog feels for his wife's lover, but for Herzog the psychological explanation will not satisfy. Herzog appears to have experienced an intimation of immortality, and his insight marks the nirvana both of the novel and of Herzog's thinking. From this point on Herzog is dragged back, at first slowly but then with increasing rapidity, into the quotidian.

In Bellow's novels the period of "intense realization" that all his heroes go through and that is always brought on by a personal crisis of one sort or another is also always either precipitated or brought to an end by a physical blow. Such is the case in *Herzog*, where, not long after his visit to his old home, Herzog is brought down to earth by a car crash in which he is slightly injured. Dazed from the accident, Herzog realizes that "his strange, spiraling flight of the last few days" (284) is over.

The progress of Herzog's consciousness ultimately leads him to the metaphysical, but this does not mean that he has no time for this world. In fact, his affirmations of life in the end appear to derive as much from his observation and experience of generous human impulses in others as from his neoreligious "feeling" that the world and its inhabitants are essentially better than they appear to be.

Is Herzog happy? The answer can perhaps be found in his description of his own consciousness as "unemployed." The phrase "unemployed consciousness" seems to be an updating of Hegel's "unhappy consciousness" (Hegel, Herzog has told us, is the philosopher who has been giving him the most trouble). The "unhappy consciousness" or "alienated soul" that Hegel describes in his *Phenomenology of Mind*—the text that Herzog has been wrestling with—aspires to be independent of the material world, to resemble God and be eternal and purely spiritual; yet at the same time it recognizes that it is part of the material world, that its physical desires and pleasures and pains are real and inescapable. As a result the "unhappy consciousness" is divided against itself. In *Herzog* contemporary holders of "unhappy consciousnesses" appear to be all those "*civilized individuals*" who "*hate and resent the civilization that makes their lives possible*" (304). In the twentieth century it is not, however, the spiritual world toward which most people aspire and against which our own world falls so miserably short, but the imaginary human situations "*invented by their own genius and which they believe is the only true and the only human reality*" (304). Herzog's consciousness, in Hegel's terms, is "happy" because he feels no pain of disjunction between what he recognizes is mortal and what he intimates of the immortal. Herzog is happy with "what is" because only through acceptance of "what is" can you receive intimations, however transient and immaterial, of what may be.

Herzog's problem is not with his happiness, in the Hegelian sense, but with his employment. What is he to do with his thoughts and ideas? What good are they? How do they help him? Are ideas a repository of human value or airy nothing? More than twenty years after writing *Herzog* Saul Bellow wrote, "There are times when I enjoy making fun of the educated American. *Herzog,* for instance, was meant to be a comic novel: a Ph.D. from a good American university falls apart when his wife leaves him for another man. . . . What is he to do in this moment of crisis, pull Aristotle and Spinoza from the shelf and storm through the pages looking for consolation and advice? The stricken man . . . becomes clearly aware of the preposterousness of such an effort."[34]

The reader of *Herzog* has a slightly different perspective. We may recognize that ideas are useless to Herzog in his immediate situation, but they are not useless to the novel either structurally or thematically. Bellow is not saying, "Don't read Spinoza or Aristotle" or "Nothing that philosophers have to say is of any importance." He is, rather, pointing to the unbalanced nature of Herzog's consciousness and to the dangers of living a life of rarified thought. Herzog's battles with great men, inadequate as they may be to the task of solving his personal problems, nevertheless enlighten us even as they fail to enlighten him.

VI

The Truth of Life

> But Shapiro's father had had no money, and peddled rotten apples from South Water Street in a wagon. There was more of the truth of life in those spotted, spoiled apples, and in old Shapiro, who smelled of the horse and of produce, than in all of these learned references. (70)

The hierarchy of value in *Herzog* does not have ideas at its head, but the key to where its most important values lie can be found in one of the ideas that Herzog cites. "*GWF Hegel (1770–1831) understood the essence of human life to be derived from history. History, memory—that is what makes us human, that, and our knowledge of death*" (162). In *The Philosophy of History,* to which Herzog is clearly referring, Hegel is interested in the way that the foundations of the human condition can be seen to change and, in his view, develop from one historical era to another. From Herzog's perspective, Hegel's ideas seem to have particular application to the lives of individuals within a single historical era and most particularly to Herzog's own life. Our sense of Herzog's "humanity" is both endorsed and increased by his moving and evocative reconstitution in his imagination of his childhood and early family life in Montreal. What is more, Herzog's memories of the characters who surrounded him—his mother, father, uncles, aunts, brothers, sister, and the family lodger—their lives, and in some cases their deaths, offer educative vignettes for the mature Herzog to reflect on. Looking back, Herzog comes to understand how much of value was enshrined in his past, and he discovers how important the past is to an understanding of his present predicament.

The importance of Herzog's nostalgic recollections of life on Napoleon Street, which fill about twenty pages almost halfway into the novel, is signaled first by a shift in Bellow's prose style that accords with a shift in Herzog's mode of consciousness. Irony, bitterness, and the sense of ideational embattlement that has characterized Herzog's discourse throughout the first third of the novel fall away when Herzog begins to describe life in the Jewish ghetto. Faced with the challenge of Herzog's past ("On Napoleon Street," Herzog tells us, "was a wider range of human feelings than he had ever again been able to find" [140]). Bellow's prose takes on a highly charged descriptive power that, aside from occasional moments of lyric intensity, he has kept in check until now. The result is the most sustained and successful piece of writing in the book.

It is possible that part of the explanation for the strength of the Napoleon Street sequence lies in the merging, at this point, of Bellow's and Herzog's autobiographies. Many of the incidents in *Herzog*—including the novel's central plot line, Herzog's betrayal by Madeleine and Gersbach—have their root in Bellow's life, and Bellow has made no secret of this. Harold Bloom has described *Herzog* as belonging to the subgenre of novels that set out to "settle scores,"[35] Bellow's targets being his third wife and Jack Ludwig his former co-editor on the ill-fated magazine *The Noble Savage*. But an ironic distance is established early in *Herzog* between the author and his protagonist; it does not powerfully undermine our reading of Herzog as Bellow's mouthpiece, but it is palpable enough to prevent us from judging Herzog's and Bellow's experience as if they were one and the same. Bellow is often poking fun at Herzog's emotional deficiencies and intellectual dependencies.

When we come to the story of Herzog's past, however, such ironic distancing between author and protagonist seems to dissipate, and the past that Bellow imagines for Herzog assumes the additional power of a personal memoir. It is worth noting that the descriptions of his childhood that Bellow has sometimes offered in his interviews and discursive prose correspond in almost every way with those of Herzog's childhood as they appear in *Herzog*.

"Napoleon Street, rotten, toylike, crazy and filthy, riddled, flogged with harsh weather—the bootlegger's boy reciting ancient prayers. To this Moses' heart was attached with great power" (140). Here is the now familiar cumulative Bellow sentence—built on five or six adjectives or adverbs, each one working to sharpen and broaden the image—that first made its appearance in *The Adventures of Augie March*. Bellow's sentences generally start to loosen up syntactically and take on their listlike appearance when he wants to communicate the abundance of an experience; Herzog's childhood is clearly formed of a set of experiences that demand such a free-style rendering.

There is both an elemental and an epic quality to Bellow's descriptions of life on Napoleon Street derived in part from the larger-than-life personalities of the individuals whom Herzog is describing but also from Bellow's decision to render the reality of Herzog's past in terms that lend to Herzog's memories something of the texture of a fable.

Shortly after the publication of *Herzog* Bellow answered an interviewer's query about his childhood thus: "I was born into a medieval ghetto in French Canada. My childhood was in ancient times which was true of all orthodox Jews. Every child was immersed in the old testament as soon as he could understand anything, so that you began life by knowing Genesis in Hebrew by heart at the age of four. You never got to distinguish between that and the other world. Later on there were translations."[36] The lack of distinction that existed in Bellow's childhood between Bible stories and daily life is surely behind the elevated prose and grand characterizations that are to be found in the Napoleon Street sequence of *Herzog*.

In addition, Herzog's stories of the past carry a biblical flavor because they, like Bible stories, emphasize what Herzog calls "a Biblical sense of personal experience and destiny" (148). The Bible is the archetypal text on which to base stories of the past peopled with colorful individuals who, despite their impoverished circumstances, view their own lives and adventures in heroic terms. "His *I* had such dignity" (149), says Herzog of his father, Jonah, who is elsewhere described as "a king." Even the name of the street that the Herzogs live on, Napoleon Street, suggests epic qualities—an imperial emotional grandeur rising out of physical squalor.

Sadly, however, contemporary experience, and in particular contemporary Jewish experience, appears to have rendered obsolete stories such as Father Herzog's. The misery that Jonah Herzog placed at the center of that tragicomic epic "the story of his life" has been made to look commonplace by the unimaginable events of the Holocaust. As Herzog puts it

> What happened during the War abolished Father Herzog's claim to exceptional suffering. We are on a more brutal standard now, a terminal standard, indifferent to persons. Part of the program of destruction into which the human spirit has poured itself with energy, even with joy. These personal histories, old tales from old times, that may not be worth remembering. . . . So many millions—multitudes—go down in terrible pain. And, at that, moral suffering is denied, these days. Personalities are good only for comic relief. (149)

Despite Herzog's reservations the entire thrust of the novel in which he is the center is to remind us that, if life is to have meaning, the individual must enjoy a salience beyond that of mere comic relief. To this end, memory, personal as well as historical, is the vital constituent in preserving our humanity.

Herzog sometimes thinks of himself as a kind of walking memory bank, and he takes pleasure in reminding his brothers and former childhood friends of tender, humorous, or dramatic moments from the past that they have forgotten. Herzog is aware that the introduction into conversation of the products of his prodigious memory often provokes embarrassment or awkwardness in his interlocutors, and he knows too that his siblings and friends are prone to view his firm hold on the past as indicative of his having a weak hold on the present or as another manifestation of his "naive," "female," "childish" uselessness. However, to the reader, Herzog's failure to repudiate the past—manifested in loving particulars like his insistence on calling his brothers by their childhood Yiddish names or in his retelling of purposeful anecdotes like those that revolve around the death of his mother—lends depth to his character, permits us to see the breadth of his sympathy and understanding, and perhaps most important, demonstrates that despite his anger and frustration of the moment he is a character who is full of love.

Moreover, Herzog's rendering of his Jewish past is not, like Valentine Gersbach's, a sick exploitation of folk memory. Gersbach makes a living by giving vastly sentimental autobiographical lectures to the Chicago Haddassah crowd, pulling heartstrings and jerking tears from an audience that he manipulates with heavy-handed schmaltz. The descriptive subtlety of Herzog's memories offers a salutary contrast to Gersbach's kitsch. Herzog's Napoleon Street is not the setting for a Canadian *Fiddler on the Roof.* Instead, the reality of life in a slum is ironically juxtaposed with the unwitting poetry of its inhabitants' aspirations. Bellow ensures that while we appreciate the effects of his subdued lyricism, we will not be lured into a false world of false feeling:

> My ancient times. Remoter than Egypt. No dawn, the foggy winters. In darkness, the bulb was lit. The stove was cold. Papa shook the grates and raised an ashen dust. The grates grumbled and squealed. The puny shovel clinked underneath. . . . The chimneys in their helmets sucked in the wind. Then the milkman came in his sleigh. The snow was spoiled and rotten with manure and litter, dead rats, dogs. The milkman in his sheepskin gave the bell a twist. It was brass like the winding key of a clock. Helen pulled the latch and went down with a pitcher for the milk. . . . The morning light could not free itself from gloom and frost. Up and down the street, the brick-recessed windows were dark, filled with darkness, and schoolgirls by twos in their black skirts walked towards the con-

> vent. And wagons, sledges, drays, the horses shuddering, the air drowned in leaden green, the dung-stained ice, trails of ashes. Moses and his brothers put on their caps and prayed together, "Ma tovu ohaleha Yaakov. . . ." "How goodly are thy tents, O Israel." (140)

The problem for Herzog lies in the distance that he now feels separates him from his past. Although he can bring the past to mind with resonance and clarity, he nevertheless senses the world of Napoleon Street as "ancient times. Remoter than Egypt." If, as Herzog tells us, he has never again been able to find such a wide range of human feelings and if, as he elsewhere insists "all he ever wanted was there" (140), it follows that he must experience his present life as narrower, emotionally curtailed, and inevitably unfulfilling.

It is made clear that contemporary life fails to measure up precisely in the area of emotional largesse when we compare the structure of the Napoleon Street sequence with that of the rest of the novel. It turns out that the "story" of Napoleon Street is in many ways paradigmatic of Herzog's current story—only with Father Herzog playing the role that is later ascribed to Moses. Napoleon Street has its Reality Instructor, Aunt Zipporah; its "foolish" protagonist, Jonah Herzog; and its loving, undemanding woman, Herzog's mother.

Jonah Herzog is a failure: he has failed in Russia in the onion importing business; failed in Canada as a farmer, a baker, and a jobber; failed in the dry-goods business and as a sack manufacturer during World War I ("when nobody else failed" [137]); failed as a junk dealer and as a marriage broker; and in the period that the Napoleon Street sequence is set, he is failing as a bootlegger. Jonah Herzog needs money, and the only person to whom he can turn is his well-off but hard and unrelenting sister Zipporah. Zipporah is a "realist," a "brilliantly shrewd woman" (145) who confronts her brother with the same kinds of facts and insights that her nephew Moses later is confronted with by his own Reality Instructors. But perhaps the most pressing of Zipporah's lessons is her reminder to Jonah Herzog that he is involved in a potentially violent business—bootlegging—but is not himself a man capable of violence. "'You can never keep up with these teamsters and butchers. Can you shoot a man?' Father Herzog was silent. 'If, God forbid, you had to shoot. . . . Could you even hit someone over the head? Come! Think it over. Answer me *gazlan*. Could you give a blow to the head?'" (145). It is worth noting in this regard that when Valentine Gersbach speaks Yiddish, he is described by Herzog as doing so with a "butcher's, teamster's, commoner's accent" (60), from which Herzog recoils.

The parallels in the lives of Moses and Jonah Herzog are clear. Valentine Gersbach is the contemporary incarnation of the low-lifes with whom Father Herzog had to struggle. Like his father before him Moses has a gun but cannot use it (the ironies accumulate when it turns out to be Father Herzog's "unused" gun that Herzog picks up with the intention of shooting Madeleine and Gersbach). Both Herzog and his father are "failures" in terms of their careers: Moses can neither apply himself to scholarship (he cannot finish the book he is writing) nor maintain a professorial position in an academic institution; Jonah cannot hold on to a job or even make a go of it as a petty criminal. These "failures," however, so glaring to the Reality Instructors who surround both Herzogs, may point to the unsuitability of the Herzogs for orthodox employment but also reveal their best qualities. The Herzogs, father and son, are committed to a life that is not eviscerated of passion and love: what they feel, they feel intensely and authentically. More to the point, their intensity of feeling, which may have periodic detrimental effects on their ability to function successfully in the outside world, is, unlike the phony sentiment of the world's Gersbachs, directed toward things that matter. "He who would do good to another must do it in Minute Particulars," says Bellow's and Herzog's favorite poet, William Blake, and in the Napoleon Street sequence when we see Father Herzog gently and considerately helping his drunken lodger Ravitch, who is covered in vomit, up the stairs to bed, we recognize the reservoir of kindness and pity that exists within his embattled soul.

The intensity with which the Herzogs throw themselves into the drama of their own lives and that produces, on the plus side, such a "wide range of human feelings" also has its negative impacts. Although the characters who surround both Jonah and Moses are either acting violently or diverting their sublimated energies into accumulating vast amounts of money or into some socially useful activity like the law or politics, the sublimations of the Herzogs are directed into moral impulses, heightened perceptions, and powerful sentiments that almost overload their sentient circuits. "All of Papa's violence went into the drama of his life, into family strife" (146), notes Herzog, while of himself he can observe, "What I seem to do is inflame myself with my own drama" (208). The result, in Herzog's case, is a kind of literal and figurative heartburn:

> Eager impulses, love, intensity, passionate dizziness that made a man sick. How long can I stand such an inner beating? The front wall of this body will go down. . . . He felt as though something terrible, inflammatory, bitter, had been grated into his bloodstream and stung and burned his veins, his face, his heart. (230–32)

Herzog's "heart condition" (the name *Herzog* contains *Herz*, the German for "heart") suggests the dangers that may be courted by a personality such as his. It is almost as if Herzog has grown sick from his own impossible nobility of feeling. The "humane feelings" that he anachronistically retains and that the Reality Instructors regard as symptoms of his terminal childishness ("Simkin . . . Edvig and Himmelstein . . . believed that in a way Herzog was rather simple, that his humane feelings were childish. That he had been spared the destruction of certain sentiments as the pet goose is spared the axe" [231]) turn out to be capable of making him sick. Herzog's disease is his essential humanity; paradoxically, it is also his salvation.

It is only from his current perspective as an adult in trouble, however, that Herzog has come to understand the value of, and to a certain extent be overwhelmed by, the past. The young Herzog whom the mature Herzog depicts on Napoleon Street and briefly after the family has moved to Chicago is, in the manner of most young and adolescent children who are busy cultivating a relationship with the broad, exuberant world around them, somewhat selfish and indifferent to the suffering of his elders. Two of the most affecting moments in Herzog's memories of his childhood and adolescence concern his refusal, through fear or distraction or both, to confront his mother's suffering and, ultimately, her death. Herzog recalls a winter scene in Montreal in the early dark of a January afternoon. His mother, dark under the eyes, breathing hard, is pulling him on a sled "over crusty ice, the tiny glitter of snow" (139). Mother and son are stopped by an old woman in a shawl: "Why are you pulling him daughter! . . . Don't sacrifice your strength to children." Herzog recalls his stubbornness: "I wouldn't get off the sled. I pretended not to understand," and comments ruefully, "One of life's hardest jobs, to make a quick understanding slow" (139).

The scene returns to Herzog's imagination when he is remembering another cold January, this one in Chicago. Herzog is sixteen and his mother is dying. "Just as when he knew she was breathless from trudging with his sled in Montreal but would not get up" (234), the adolescent Herzog again allows his mother to comfort him when it is she who needs the attention. Herzog is busy with schoolwork, deep into Spengler's *The Decline of the West,* his mother comes into his room and admonishes him not to work so late and in such poor light. She looks terrible and the message of her appearance is "*My son this is death*" (234). Once again, the mature Herzog notes the evasion of his younger self: "I chose not to read this text." The irony here, and its relation to Herzog's current crisis, is instructive. Herzog can easily immerse himself in the abstract ideas contained in written texts, but he tends to evade or avoid the "texts of life," the concrete realities that confront him. It is hardly, at age sixteen, a major crime not to be able to confront the death of one's own mother, but the mature Herzog recognizes that his engaging in ideological battles with texts must not substitute for but rather complement his establishment of an unmediated relationship to life and death—one that incorporates learning how to face death without being governed by it. Herzog chides himself for having been a "bookish, callow boy" (235); the mature Herzog, more experienced but still bookish, is trying to "come to better terms with death" (232).

What does it mean to "come to better terms with death"? In Herzog's case, the guilt that he feels when he remembers his evasion of his mother's death urges him to remind himself to look at life more squarely in the face, while at the same time his memories of his mother's painful submission to her fate prompt him to hope that "such melancholy" and "sadness" will not be "perpetuated." "When we come to better terms with death," says Herzog, "we'll wear a different expression, we human beings. Our looks will change. *When* we come to terms" (232). Herzog's hope once again appears to be infused with some form of transcendent faith—a faith that is tempting to view as yet another "evasion" but one that is as awkward to disdain as genuine faith.

In a fascinating way, Herzog's adult relation to death is foreshadowed in an incident that he remembers from his early childhood. Herzog recalls asking his mother, at age six, how Adam was created from the dust of the ground. Sarah Herzog responds by rubbing the palm of her hand with her finger until "a particle of what certainly looked like earth . . . appeared on the deep lined skin." Herzog's offers the memory as an example of one of the rare moments when his mother did not "lie to spare his feelings" and muses that his mother offered him this "proof partly in the spirit of comedy. The wit you can have only when you consider death very plainly" (232). The message that Sarah Herzog has conveyed, of course, has less to do with how Adam was created than with how we die. "Dust to dust" being the hidden text of her reply. As we have seen, Herzog refuses to incorporate this message (chooses "not to read this text") into his consciousness until much later in his life, by which time he has developed the hope that a radical spiritual transformation may improve his relations with the inevitable.

Interestingly, Herzog's earliest conscious confrontation with knowledge of death is precipitated in precisely the same manner as Freud's as it is described in Ernest Jones's biography. Perhaps the palm-rubbing trick was a piece of folklore known to mothers all over the European Jewish world or perhaps Bellow simply incorporated an experience of Freud's into that of his hero's, but in uncannily similar fashion Jones reports that Freud's first confrontation with the inevitability of death occurred at age six when his mother responded to a question (on what subject, we do not know, but given that Hebrew school begins for Jewish children at age six and commences with the study of Genesis, we might guess that Freud's question was also Creation related) "by rubbing her hands together and showing him the dark fragments of epidermis that came there as a specimen of the earth we are made of."[37] For young Freud, the message that "thou owest nature a death"[38] is one that he reluctantly acquiesces to. For Herzog, in contrast, the resistance is long-term. The reactions of the two six-year-olds, one real, one fictional, to the most real of reality principles reveals, at its earliest stage, the conflict between Freud and Bellow over whether what "we do not know" has a "natural" or "metaphysical" character. For Freud and Bellow both, or Freud and Herzog both, facing the reality of death is paramount to both the health and humanity of the individual. But to Freud that "facing" must be unillusioned, the reality must be accepted in a natural form undistorted by the intrusion of metaphysical speculation. For Bellow and Herzog, it seems unlikely that we can "come to terms with death" *without* the aid of some as yet unidentified transforming metaphysical agent.

The importance of life on Napoleon Street as a crucible of value and meaning is underscored in the Napoleon Street sequence by Bellow's vivid characterizations. It is no accident that the characters that Herzog brings up, fully imagined, out of his "ancient past" seem to have more life in them and a greater presence for the reader than many of the characters who are Herzog's contemporaries. Not even Herzog's "good brother" Will, or his friend, Luke Asphalter, both of whom asseverate an appropriately large number of the human virtues, have the characterological substantiality of Mama, Papa, and Aunt Zipporah. Bellow seems to be making a point about the effects of the culture on individual personality. Herzog's contemporaries are attenuated in comparison with their immediate forbears. They have lost something of the stuff of life. As the epigraph to this chapter suggests, the "learned references" of Shapiro *fils* have less of "the truth of life" than the "spotted spoiled apples" of Shapiro *père* (70).

This sense of generational decline permeates many of Bellow's novels. There is a noticeable disparity between the dynamic way in which Bellow chooses to characterize his first-generation Jewish immigrants, who uniformly display a wholeness of being, and his characterization of his protagonists and their contemporaries, who are altogether more fragmented personalities. In *The Victim,* for example, or *The Adventures of Augie March,* we come across characters like the old Yiddish journalist Schlossberg or Grandma Lausch and William Einhorn—individuals who are painted in bold strokes that reflect the self-knowledge and self-assurance that they manifest. These characters have a palpable presence in the novels in which they appear as opposed to Bellow's somewhat insubstantial protagonists like Asa Leventhal in *The Victim* or Augie March or even Herzog himself. As a result we tend to extrapolate Bellow's central figures as "talking heads" rather than as fully rounded personalities. "Modern character," says Herzog, "is inconstant, divided, vacillating" (107), and Bellow's chosen modes of characterization seem to indicate that he agrees.

Still, Herzog knows that such "truth of life" as he found invested in old Shapiro will not come back and that although his childhood past remains a deep well of meaning and value, drawing from it alone cannot sustain him through his present crisis.

Herzog portrays himself as a disintegrating personality in a rapidly disintegrating universe. Everywhere around Herzog things are falling apart. What is the difference between Herzog's position and the grim nihilism of the Reality Instructors? To begin with, it seems possible that in his current unbalanced state Herzog's vision has become somewhat selective. Bellow has put the pathetic fallacy to work in this novel, and Herzog's moods are often projected onto or reflected in the environment that he inhabits. When Herzog takes the cab in Manhattan that begins his fruitless journey to Martha's Vineyard, he winds up in a traffic jam in the garment district: the noise from the machinists working in the lofts comes across to him "as though clothes were being torn not sown" (32). When Herzog steps out of his Manhattan apartment on his way to spend an evening with Ramona, his attention is caught by a wrecking crew destroying an apartment building. When he goes to the movies, it is to see an Indian film; the fate of a poor old

Indian woman and her young daughter brings tears to Herzog's eyes because he cannot separate his response to the characters from thoughts of his own mother and daughter. When Herzog opens the paper, it is to read of Soviet astronauts disintegrating in space; when he contemplates the universe, it is exploding novae that have his attention; and so on. We are made aware that Herzog, probably quite unconsciously, is searching out an external world to reflect his inner state.

What is most interesting, however, is the way in which Herzog is sometimes able to transform what he observes of disintegration into an uplifting experience. Herzog is sensitive to what he calls "unexpected intrusions of beauty" (218), and he is often able to discover an aesthetic quality in his experiences to balance the sense of universal disintegration that the experience is reinforcing. The work of the wrecking crew is a case in point.

> The great metal ball swung at the walls, passed easily through brick, and entered the rooms, the lazy weight browsing on kitchens and parlors. Everything it touched wavered and burst, spilled down. There rose a white tranquil cloud of plaster dust. The afternoon was ending, and in the widening area of demolition was a fire, fed by the wreckage. Moses heard the air, softly pulled towards the flames, felt the heat. The workmen, heaping the bonfire with wood, threw strips of molding like javelins. Paint and varnish smoked like incense. The old flooring burned gratefully—the funeral of exhausted objects. Scaffolds walled with pink, white, green doors quivered as the six-wheeled trucks carried off fallen brick. The sun, now leaving for New Jersey and the west, was surrounded by a dazzling broth of atmospheric gases. Herzog observed that people were spattered with red stains, and that he himself was flecked on the arms and chest. He crossed Seventh Avenue and entered the subway. (175)

Here, the harsh urban landscape is transformed by Herzog's lyric vision into an event at once beautiful, mysterious, and oddly weightless. The "red stains" that cover the Seventh Avenue crowd can be read either as symbols of woundedness, concomitant with the general sense of things going down (the building, the sun) that the scene conveys, or in more positive fashion, as emanations from the sun, which Herzog soon after describes as "the spot that inoculated us against the whole of disintegrating space" (241). The "going down" may be inevitable, but it is not necessarily a painful crash: the brick and mortar of the apartment building "wavers," "bursts," and "spills"; the scaffolding "quivers"; the paint and varnish send up not toxic fumes but smoke like "incense"; the old flooring is "grateful" to burn; the sun on the Jersey shore is not obscured by a haze of pollutants but "surrounded by a dazzling broth of atmospheric gases." Herzog's "wasteland" is not, like T. S. Eliot's, a metaphoric representation of the sterility, vulgarity, and decadence of contemporary life, but an environment that cryptically signals the existence of hidden beauty and transcendent meaning: entropy, like dying, appears to maintain a potential for transformation, for being accepted "on better terms."

My invocation of T. S. Eliot at this point is not arbitrary, for Herzog's first step after witnessing the wrecking crew in action is to descend into the Seventh Avenue subway. Unlike the speaker of Eliot's *Four Quartets,* for whom the descent into the London underground is a journey down into a contemporary ring of Dante's Inferno where the individuals riding the circle line are characterized by facelessness and alienation, Herzog's experience in the subway leads him dizzily to a moment of affirmation. As he passes through the turnstile, Herzog "drops his fare in the slot where he saw a whole series of tokens lighted from within and magnified by the glass. Innumerable millions of passengers had polished the wood of the turnstile with their hips. From this arose a feeling of communion—brotherhood in one of its cheapest forms" (176). Herzog's Manhattan may be as dilapidated as Eliot's war-scarred London, but the fictional character's and the poet's respective interpretations of the signs in their environment are quite different.

Are Herzog's intimations of the existence of a transcendent community to be trusted? Herzog himself is unsure whether he is perceiving or projecting—and probably he is doing both. Certainly, the doors of perception have opened wide for Herzog, and unlike Aldous Huxley, they have done so for him without the aid of chemical agents. Even so, Herzog seems aware that what he sees in the world may be only a reflection of his own desires.

> In these days of near delirium and wide-ranging disordered thought, deeper currents of feeling had heightened his perceptions, or made him instill something of his own into his surroundings. As though he painted them with moisture and color taken from his own mouth, his blood, liver, bowels, genitals. (278)

Early in the novel Herzog has described himself as a "prisoner of perception," "a compulsory witness" who cannot help but observe the "too exciting" details of life with the utmost intensity (72). What is interesting is the way in which Herzog's "heightened perceptions," brought on by internal and external chaos, produce moments of powerful lyric intensity. In his heightened state of being Herzog becomes witness to a charged beauty that ultimately overrides the exigencies of the unpleasant experience that has spawned it. In this way, Herzog's aesthetic experiences accommodate a transforming power that enables Herzog to diminish or render commonplace his crises of the quotidian.

An exemplary moment in this regard comes when Madeleine announces to Herzog that they must separate and that Herzog must leave their home immediately. Herzog has been outside working in his backyard enjoying the common beauty of the day: "The first frost had already caught the tomatoes. The grass was dense and soft, with the peculiar beauty it gains when the cold days come and the gossamers lie on it in the morning; the dew is thick and lasting. The tomato vines had blackened and the red globes had burst" (8). Madeleine calls Herzog into the house. She is dressed and made up as if for a dramatic performance—as Herzog points out, she is not Pontritter the "American Stanislavsky's" daughter for nothing. The shock and success of Madeleine's theatrically contrived moment jolts Herzog into one of his heightened states of perception:

> In the window on glass shelves there stood an ornamental collection of small glass bottles, Venetian and Swedish. They came with the

> house. The sun now caught them. They were pierced with the light. Herzog saw the waves, the threads of color, the spectral intersecting bars, and especially a great blot of flaming white on the center of the wall above Madeleine. She was saying, "We can't live together any more." (9)

On one level, Herzog is merely experiencing here the familiar distraction and shock of anyone who suddenly finds his life turned upside down. But Herzog's almost hallucinatory vision is also suggestive of his ability to "rise above" the unpleasant situations that he finds himself in and become infused with what can only be called a "transcendental light"—and this despite the fact that Herzog, Bellow, and Bellow's readers recognize that to admit the possibility of such an auroral glow is potentially embarrassing in late twentieth-century North America. Does the light come from the outside or from the inside? Neither Herzog nor Bellow resolve this question. There is little evidence in the novel to suggest that Herzog is not wildly projecting his transcendental yearnings onto indifferent nature. For example, the "prisoner of perception" describes his Berkshire lawn thus:

> Formed like a large teardrop of green, it had a gray elm at its small point, and the bark of the huge tree, dying of dutch blight, was purplish gray. Scant leaves for such a vast growth. An oriole's nest, in the shape of a gray heart, hung from twigs. God's veil over things makes them all riddles. If they were not all so particular, detailed, and very rich I might have more rest from them. But I am a prisoner of perception. (72)

Melancholy, oboe-playing Herzog sees his lawn in the shape of a "teardrop" and the oriole's nest in the shape of a "gray heart": these shapes, we might surmise, are not so much God's riddles as the shapes of Herzog's feelings. Yet, as often as not, Herzog's heightened awareness of the external world does not narcissistically refer him back to himself but rather spurs him to the kind of affirmation of brotherhood and community that was inspired by his trip down into the Seventh Avenue subway.

It seems possible to solve God's riddle on Herzog's behalf. The riddle carries the message that the invisible community, harmony, and humanity of the world—especially invisible to the embattled Herzog surrounded, as he is, by hypocrisy, betrayal, and crass materialism—is signaled in the unexpected intrusions of beauty thrown up in Herzog's path from time to time. This beauty, while it may be mistaken for and may even contain the projections of Herzog's aesthetic sensibility, is also imbued with its own mysterious power—an aesthetic quality that inspires moral reflection. The "moral reflection" rider is an important one, for it is clear that a "pure" aesthetic experience is of only fleeting interest to Herzog.

Skeptical readers will view those moments of transcendent apprehension that lead Herzog to affirm the value of community as all too convenient compensations for the absence of real community that Herzog experiences in his life. It is also tempting to apply such skepticism to Herzog's reconstitution in memory of his "ancient times." Herzog is clearly much more successful at forming a community in his head than in the society that he inhabits.

Although Herzog is undoubtedly neurotic and his forays into the past and his passing moments of spiritual illumination may indeed be "therapeutic," it seems unnecessarily reductive to deny them value in any other terms. To refuse Herzog the authenticity of his ecstatic moments of social communion or his aesthetically founded spiritual apprehensions except as elements in a "cure" for his "disease" is, ultimately, to deny the value of aspiration and hope for humankind.

Midway through the novel, Herzog recalls a speech that he gave as class orator at his high school in 1934. His chosen text is Emerson: "*Let it be granted,*" he reads, "*that our life, as we lead it, is common and mean. . . . Beautiful and perfect men we are not now. . . . The community in which we live will hardly bear to be told that every man should be open to ecstasy or divine illumination*" (160). To be, like Emerson, "in earnest about beauty and perfection" is, Herzog believes, "a thoroughly American credential" (160). Moreover, there seems no doubt that Herzog believes in God (he says as much), although what Herzog calls God is clearly not the Jehovah of the Old Testament. Perhaps God as a life "open to ecstasy or divine illumination" is about as close as we can get to defining the source of Herzog's belief system, and in this formulation Herzog's spirituality can usefully be regarded as a brand of American optimism.

Herzog may not have a traditional God, but he does have a traditional religious affiliation, for whatever the content of his "beliefs" Herzog remains unequivocably Jewish. Herzog's Jewishness, in fact, appears to be an important aspect of his being, although any attempts to analyze in what ways this is so quickly run into trouble. Herzog's Jewishness, on the surface, doesn't seem to have anything to do with his spiritual feelings: he doesn't practice his religion, he describes synagogues as "suffocating" (316), and he is often to be found (as, for example, when in the company of Sono Oguki) relishing his release from the constraints of his orthodox upbringing. There is much discussion of things Jewish in *Herzog,* but no real sense of conflict or problem is engendered. Herzog's Jewishness appears as one aspect of a wholly individual being; it is not a condition that transcends his private situation. Herzog is a Jew, an academic, and an intellectual, but the order of these terms can be felt as quite arbitrary.

It is tempting to read *Herzog,* though, as enlarging on a traditional Jewish theme: the wise fool simultaneously cherished and despised by his worldly people of whose special destiny he is an impossible yet essential ideal. But this theme is not at the center of the novel. The center is occupied unambiguously by the unique condition of Herzog himself in his individuality. The role of Jewish wise fool is one that Herzog finds himself playing, but he contemplates it wryly and with amusement as of him but not constituting him.

In what ways, then, is Herzog's Jewishness important to him and to us? Many critics have looked to the style of Herzog's consciousness, which reflects the style of Bellow's writing (a style in which, as Bellow himself once admiringly noted of Montaigne, he can "pass with ease from kitchen matters to metaphysics"[39]) to provide an answer. It is in the mixture of high and low thoughts (both author's and protagonists)—the Jew with his head in the clouds and his feet in mud—that a recognizably Jewish attitude is to be discovered. Bellow certainly draws on the familiar mingling of the high and low in Yiddish literature, and he even adopts as models for his characters some stock figures from Yiddish folktales, but there is something more profoundly Jewish to his writing—and to Moses Herzog's behavior.

In a review that Bellow once wrote of a book by Sholem Aleichem, he connected the strength of Yiddish literature and the wit and brilliance of Jewish storytelling throughout history to the unhappy peculiarities of the Jewish historical position:

> Powerlessness appears to force people to have recourse to words. Hamlet has to unpack his heart with words, he complains. The fact that the Jews of Eastern Europe lived among menacing and powerful neighbors no doubt contributed to the subtlety and the richness of the words with which they unpacked.[40]

It is important not to confuse the above with any notion of Bellow's promoting suffering as ennobling. As Herzog points out in an unmailed letter to Professor Mermelstein, "*suffering breaks people, crushes them, and is simply unilluminating*" (317). Bellow is talking about the potential for language, particularly in storytelling, to garner an impressive power of its own when it is paradoxically generated by external impotence. The Jews of Europe were obliged to live by the credo held in Isaac Babel's famous line that "No steel can pierce the human heart so chillingly as a period at the right moment." Moses Herzog, it will be remembered, also senses himself as powerless. He is not denied social freedoms in the manner of his ancestors, but he is without influence, it seems, in matters relating to both his private and public destinies. What Herzog does have is his "story," and he too unpacks his heart with words. As Bellow has elsewhere pointed out—in reference to Hamlet's dying request of Horatio to "tell my story": "In defeat, a story contains the hope of vindication, of justice. The storyteller is able to make others accept his version of things."[41]

This is precisely Herzog's endeavor. As he tells Lucas Asphalter, "I go after reality with language. Perhaps I'd like to change it all into language, to force Madeleine and Gersbach to have a *conscience*. . . . I conjure up a whole environment and catch them in the middle. I put my whole heart into these constructions. But they are constructions" (272). It is Herzog's faith in and reliance on the transforming power of language that is perhaps the most Jewish thing about him. Herzog may not be able to pull the trigger and shoot Madeleine and Gersbach, but he can settle scores just as effectively using the weapons of Isaac Babel.

VII

Pattern and Structure

When *Herzog* was first published, some critics complained that the novel was unstructured—and the complaints have continued on and off over the decades. The fact that Bellow produced the 340-page novel from some six thousand pages of manuscript should give us some indication of the thought that went into the book and renders it unlikely that, as Tony Tanner suggested back in 1965, the novel is "as mismanaged and patternless as its hero's life."[42] In any case, Herzog's life may be mismanaged, but it is not patternless. In fact, the structure and plot of the novel reinforce and repeat the unmistakably dialectical pattern of Herzog's behavior and thought.

Herzog is caught between his desire for order and his propensity to create chaos; his tendency toward stasis and his yearning for action; equilibrium and a kind of mental staggering; internal harmony and neurotic nervousness. Herzog's greatest desire is to arrive at some kind of synthesis of being (if not of understanding), but the project is one that he also views ironically. At the end of *Herzog,* Herzog does appear to have achieved an approximate resolution of his problems, although the transcendent silence that he enacts in the Berkshires has not always satisfied readers.

Herzog looks "patternless" because the structure is complex. For much of the novel Herzog is remembering himself in the act of remembering. We thus follow flashbacks within flashbacks. When we are introduced to Herzog, he is at his country house in Ludeyville in the western part of Massachusetts; he is alone, musing on the recent and not-so-recent past, and waiting for his brother, Will, to come and visit him. Our sojourn in the Berkshires does not last long. Within a page and a half we have entered the first flashback and joined Herzog on the couch of his Seventeenth Street kitchenette in Manhattan. Here he enters into a long series of reminiscences on the breakup of his marriage and all its attendant follies. The action proceeds in New York, onto Chicago, and eventually to the Berkshires. Throughout the novel Herzog's activities are interspersed with memories, and some, like those that return Herzog to his early childhood, take the form of extended flashbacks.

When we are twenty-five pages from the end of the novel, the opening line of the text, "If I am out of my mind, it's all right with me" (315), pops into Moses Herzog's head, and we know that Bellow has signaled a return to our place of departure. From here on, everything happens in the "present" of the novel. This "present"—the week and a half that Herzog spends in the Berkshires—occupies only a small fraction of the text, which is dominated by Herzog's remembering of memories. However, we begin and end with Herzog at rest and at peace with himself. All the agitation of the intervening pages is thus bracketed and contained, and in this way the structure reinforces our sense of Herzog's contentment and suggests that it is now impregnable.

Within the flashbacks and reminiscences that constitute the bulk of the text, we can discern Bellow building plot and creating structure in a series of dialectical movements that are variations on the Hegelian prime triad. Whether it is the development of Herzog's amorous history or his passing from one environmental setting to another, the pyramidal pattern is the same and can be used to exemplify, let us say, a movement from order to chaos (thesis and antithesis), which terminates in a third and more adequate stage (the synthesis) in which, say, order is discovered but without boredom in attendance. This synthesis, however, does not bring the dialectical process to a stop but, inadequate in some fresh way, serves as the thesis for a new dialectical movement.

Three of the most important women in Herzog's life are his first two wives, Daisy and Madeleine, and his current girlfriend, Ramona. Daisy, Herzog tell us, offered him all the comforts of an honest, bourgeois housewife—"stability, symmetry, order, containment were Daisy's strength" (126). But life with Daisy is dull and uninspiring, and Herzog eventually leaves her: "What actually happened? I gave up the shelter of an orderly, purposeful, lawful existence because it bored me, and I felt it was simply a slacker's life" (103).

Herzog recognizes that he has "treated [Daisy] miserably" (14), but he wants a life that is a little less ordinary. He finds one with Madeleine, who is Daisy's antithesis in every way. Madeleine is a great architect of chaos: she bounces checks, refuses to clean up the Herzog house, tears Herzog's new shirts up to use them as cleaning rags, and, on top of everything else, she has an affair with Herzog's best friend. Madeleine is irresponsible and extravagant, and after the first flush of passion has worn off in their relationship, Herzog soon discovers that some yearning for order in his life (although not Daisy's suffocating brand) has returned. "Jesus Christ," Herzog cries, as the delivery trucks roll up to the door laden with "jewelry, cigarette boxes, coats and dresses, lamps and carpets" (56), "we've got to have a little order in these surroundings" (124). Herzog becomes Madeleine's victim just as Daisy has been Herzog's.

From Herzog's perspective, although he is more in love with Madeleine than he ever was with Daisy, neither woman approximates a satisfactory partner. What Herzog appears to need, and appears to find, is a personality who combines Daisy's order with Madeleine's alluringly fiery and dramatic character. Herzog finds Ramona. Of Ramona we learn "[s]he thought she could restore order and sanity to his [Herzog's] life, and if she did that it would be logical to marry her. Or, in her style, he would desire to be united with her. And it would be a union that really unified. Tables, beds, parlors, money, laundry.

and automobile, culture and sex knit into one web" (185). Ramona does indeed look like the answer to Herzog's problems; she is responsible, productive (she runs her own business well enough to drive a Mercedes), *and* up for adventure and sexy. Looks, it should be pointed out, don't come into it; Herzog's women, like all the women attached to Bellow's protagonists, are, as Irving Howe has described them, "tiresomely beautiful."[43]

But Herzog is not planning to marry Ramona. Indeed, at the end of the novel her presence in his life is beginning to make him feel a little uncomfortable, uncomfortable enough for the reader to suspect that she may not last long once Herzog has completed his recuperation. Ramona's shortcomings are her thinly veiled desperation to be married and her overly theoretical commitment to sex. Herzog has had enough of "ideas" and perhaps is searching for someone a little less burdened and a little more spontaneous than Ramona. But this is the "thesis" for Herzog's next dialectical movement—one that we are not to witness in the novel.

The three environments that Herzog inhabits most frequently in the novel—Manhattan, Chicago, and the Berkshires—function in similar manner to Herzog's three main women. In addition to being conjured realistically with Bellow's usual skill, evocative power, and enlightening attention to detail, they are also symbolic nodes in Herzog's emotional and intellectual landscape.

During a dinner conversation with Ramona, Herzog points, quite unconsciously, to the different elements of his personality that come into play in New York and Chicago. Herzog is discussing George Hoberly, Ramona's discarded lover. Hoberly hangs around outside Ramona's apartment hoping to catch a glimpse of her and also in order to keep tabs on Herzog. Herzog recognizes Hoberly as a kind of "double" who is playing the same role in relation to Ramona that Herzog himself plays for Madeleine and Gersbach. Herzog spells out the identification to Ramona. "I think that it's while in New York I am the man inside, in Chicago the man in the street is me" (199). Herzog is referring only to the similarity of their respective positions as jilted lovers, but to the reader, and perhaps Bellow intended it this way, Herzog's words also serve as an appropriate description of the way in which a sense of Herzog's divided self is communicated by the perceptible difference of his behavior in New York and Chicago. In New York "the man inside" appears to be in the ascendancy, while in Chicago Herzog is very much "the man in the street."

In Manhattan, for the most part, Herzog is supine on a couch or sitting in the back of a cab or in a subway car or train. His primary activities are thinking and meditating—communing with himself in one way or another. By contrast, Herzog in Chicago is all motion. He rushes from his former home on Harper Avenue in the suburbs to his friend Luke Asphalter's house; he pays a quick visit to his stepmother and retrieves his father's old gun; he returns to Harper Avenue; he leaves almost immediately to visit Phoebe Gersbach; he goes back to Asphalter to pick up his daughter and take her to the aquarium. On his Chicago minijourneys Herzog doesn't have time for much deep thought; his talk is largely made up of dialogue with others rather than conversation with himself. He drives rather than being driven; he even gets into a car crash and experiences the local drama of a visit to the police station.

The symbolic alternatives of New York and Chicago appear to be between stasis and motion, inactivity and activity, and contemplation or action. At least, the way in which the novel is structured as a tale of two cities heightens our awareness of these antithetical forces in Herzog's being. However, the tale of two cities also incorporates a house in the country, and Herzog's life in the Berkshires both repeats and appears to resolve his internal conflicts much as Ramona repeats and appears to resolve elements and conflicts in the Daisy/Madeleine configuration.

Herzog's Berkshire house, which he has bought with $20,000 of his father's hard-earned money, is in a place called Ludeyville, which, Herzog tells us, is "not on the Esso map" (329). Herzog spends a year of his marriage in this symbolically uncharted territory after Madeleine has convinced him to give up his academic post and become an independent scholar. Madeleine is pregnant, and at first, all is rosy. Herzog throws himself into fixing up the house: "with hysterical passion he painted, patched, tarred gutters, plastered holes. . . . A year of work saved the house from collapse" (120).

The Ludeyville house itself (Ludeyville suggesting both *loony* and *ludens* to the reader; Herzog calls it "Herzog's folly" [309] where the undercurrent of mild madness is equally present) appears to be a symbolic extension of Herzog's state of mind: can he put his broken life together with Madeleine? From the outside he appears to be successful, but then things start to go wrong. Madeleine beings to exhibit signs of paranoia (she thinks that Herzog has hired a private detective to follow her), and not long after the birth of their daughter, Junie, she commences (unbeknown to Herzog) her seven-year affair with Gersbach. Madeleine, as has been noted, brings domestic chaos to Herzog's life, and it is his job to keep things together. Herzog's work begins to suffer, he is having trouble with Hegel, but that is probably the least of his troubles. In the face of Madeleine's onslaught "the inner man" who reserves mornings for "brainwork" fails to get anything done, and the "man in the street" slowly lets the house fall apart again. In Herzog's memories of his life in the Berkshires, we see reproduced both the unemployed consciousness of New York and the spurious activity of Chicago. Herzog, it seems, has trouble in holding himself together in the place where the deeply antithetical elements in his personality are equally foregrounded.

However, Herzog's return to the Berkshires after all the action has gone by reveals him, and the place that he is inhabiting, in a new light—literally as well as metaphorically as Mr. Tuttle, the local handyman or "miracle man" (339), manages to get electricity restored to the run-down old house in double-quick time. In Herzog's second incarnation in the Berkshires he is able to come to terms with everything and everyone who has been troubling him.

A late twentieth-century Jewish Thoreau, Herzog wanders his twenty acres of woodlot feeling at peace and joyful. He forgives Madeleine and Gersbach, stops his quarreling with dead philosophers, and resolves to commit himself to the life of whatever community he finds himself a part of: "I mean to share with other human beings as far as possible and not destroy my remaining years in the same way"

(322). "*Hineni*," says Herzog to himself—"here I am" (310), Moses' answer to God when God calls him from the burning bush—and Herzog seems to be responding to an idea of God made manifest in the world. The beauty of his physical surroundings, an acceptance of the vicissitudes of life, an accommodation with death—Herzog significantly leaves undisturbed the bones of some dead birds that have nested in an abandoned toilet bowl and been trapped under the seat—Herzog in the Berkshires experiences a moment of profound internal resolution.

> I look at myself and see chest, thighs, feet—a head. This strange organization, I know it will die. And inside—something, something, happiness . . . "Thou movest me." That leaves no choice. Something produces intensity, a holy feeling. . . . This intensity, doesn't it mean anything? Is it an idiot joy that makes this animal . . . exclaim something? And he thinks this reaction a sign, a proof, of eternity? . . . "Thou movest me." But what do you want Herzog? But that's just it—not a solitary thing. I am pretty well satisfied to be, to be just as it is willed, and for as long as I remain in occupancy. (340)

Some critics have discovered in Herzog's Berkshires transcendence a complacency or quietism that is disturbing. But Herzog's resolution is all internal, an acceptance of self and a celebration of life from which we cannot infer that Herzog thinks that we should cease to worry about famine in Africa or corruption in domestic politics. In Herzog's own life too there is still a great deal of confusion, and at the end of the novel we can by no means be sure that Herzog's newfound state will assist him more than minimally in avoiding the kind of trouble that he is prone to fall into. We do not see Herzog lead the communal life that he intends to, just as we do not see the resolution of his ambivalent feelings for Ramona. Herzog's theoretical "synthesis" in the Berkshires, in the absence of an accompanying praxis, remains incomplete. Herzog still has a long way to go, but at least he has arrived in a position, which we might usefully call creative stasis, from which he can prepare to begin again.

The above examples, in the areas of character and setting, of the way in which the dynamics of *Herzog* rest on a dialectical structure are striking but should not be misconstrued as indications of rigid schematism in Bellow's text. It is true that in two of his more recent novels, *Mr. Sammler's Planet* and *The Dean's December,* Bellow's characters have lacked individuation and appear to have been mechanically created in order to accommodate and foreground Bellow's polemical and political ideas. But in *Herzog* the protagonist and those who surround him are idiosyncratic enough not to invite categorization as mouthpieces of the author, and they accrue an interest far beyond that of the symbolic.

Interestingly, however, the structure of the individual characters in *Herzog,* their characterological makeup, corresponds to the structure of the novel as a whole. Characters who appear to be neatly and irrevocably divided personalities (at least as described by Herzog) are, by the end of the novel, permitted (again by Herzog) to transcend themselves in some manner and emerge, happily, as more than the sum of their characteristics. An insistence that a human being is "more than his 'characteristics'" (366) is of course the grounds of Herzog's climactic insight into the human personality. This insight, which he applied to himself when standing in a Western Union office at Blackstone and 53rd in Chicago, now turns out to have more general application and to include even Madeleine and Gersbach.

For much of the novel Madeleine and Gersbach are described by Herzog in uncompromising terms as characters defined by antithetical, but equally unpalatable, qualities. Herzog describes Madeleine as "proud but not well-wiped," "beautiful but distorted by rage," "a mixed mind of pure diamond and Woolworth glass," and "as sweet as cheap candy, and just as reminiscent of poison as chemical sweet acids" (299). There is no room for warmth of any kind in Herzog's descriptions of Madeleine, and the cold-hearted aspects of her personality are revealed in the narrative in the way in which she goes about conducting her affair with Gersbach. Gersbach himself comes in for even rougher treatment, and where issues of his character are engaged, Bellow helps Herzog's case along with the use of a few handy literary devices: Gersbach's first name is "Valentine," which suggests the cloying sentimentality of which he is capable; he has flaming red hair and one good leg, both of which are conventional literary signals, at least they were in the nineteenth-century novel, that someone diabolic is present. Herzog cannot be accused of "projecting" either Gersbach's name or his hair or his leg onto him; these qualities are Bellow's doing. Of course, it is all Bellow's doing, but unmediated external description is not distorted by Herzog's point of view.

Gersbach's treatment of Herzog is, on the surface, unspeakable. The ugliest thing about him is his hypocrisy, revealed most damningly in the way in which he continues to act as Herzog's sympathetic listening board and ostensible go-between even while he is actively engaged as Madeleine's lover. In this respect, the low point in Gersbach's behavior arrives when he comes to Herzog's house to remove Madeleine's possessions and pockets her diaphragm while Herzog naively looks on. It is hardly surprising, given his behavior, that Herzog describes Gersbach as a "psychopath" (298) and discerns in him a resemblance to "Putzi Haenfstaengl, Hitler's own pianist" (19). However, the reader understands that the extremism of Herzog's descriptions has been inspired by jealousy, pain, and anger. The observable reality of Gersbach corresponds more accurately with Herzog's descriptions of him as a "charlatan . . . with hot phony eyes" (298) or a "loud, flamboyant, ass-clutching brute" (102). But there is also, Herzog decides, another more human Gersbach who must be acknowledged: the Gersbach whom Herzog sees tenderly bathing Junie. By the end of the novel, as Herzog grows calmer, he beings to acknowledge the extent of his own projections. Madeleine, for all her bitchery, Herzog decides is a "good mother," and there is even something to celebrate in the quality of her high-strung performance. In the final accounting of character both Madeleine and Gersbach are seen to escape definition through either Herzog's vituperation or Bellow's not-so-subtle symbol making. Madeleine may "read three or four murder mysteries a week" (73) and have the habit of looking "at her reflection in a knife blade ("*Will never understand what women want.*" . . . "*They eat green salad and drink human blood*" [41–42]), but her murderous instincts—according to Herzog she is forever trying to "do him in"

(4)—are repressed and she is a comic not a threatening figure. Herzog finally decides that, like himself, Madeleine and Gersbach are finally "unknowable." They resist his definitions even as he resists theirs, and thus evading categorization they are able to embody not only the "truth" that Herzog comes to—that individuals are more than the sum of their characteristics—but also his more general assertion that "utter clarity of explanation . . . is false" (194).

Why should we accept Herzog's revisionist characterizations of his antagonists? The novel as a whole can only endorse Herzog's hard-won "benign" view of those who surround him by making us aware of the extent to which, up until the end of the novel, Herzog has been an unreliable narrator. We tend to accept that Herzog's last-minute judgments of Madeleine and Gersbach are accurate—they are not so bad after all—only because Herzog seems to make them after he has recovered his mental balance.

In similar fashion, Bellow cannot suddenly change the physical appearances of characters that carry with them certain symbolic associations when Herzog changes his mind about them—Gersbach will always have a limp and red hair—but he can make us see, perhaps, that *our* associations carry symbolic weight only when we are buying heavily into Herzog's selective version of things. Madeleine and Gersbach are "diabolic" only when Herzog says that they are: Mady has "the will of a demon" (102), and Gersbach's appearance and behavior are Mephistophelean (215). But the reality is that Madeleine and Gersbach are no more twinned Mephistophelean figures than Herzog is the Faust that some critics have taken him to be. Cheating, betrayal, and hypocrisy are not exactly capital crimes, and Herzog himself, as many readers often overlook, has actually cheated on his wives too. Moreover, the distinction between real crime and real horror as they exist in the world and the painful but pathetic "crimes against Herzog" is made quite clear in the courtroom scene that Herzog witnesses.

Herzog, we will remember, in his heightened emotional state, associates the mother and her lover who have murdered their child with Madeleine and Gersbach and their maltreatment of Junie: they locked the child in a car while they were having an argument. The strength of Herzog's association is probably increased by a physical coincidence: the female defendant in the case has red hair and wears an orthopedic boot.

However, the two mother/lover/child triangles have little in common beyond surface details. The reader is immediately aware of this, but Herzog, because he is emotionally charged, vulnerable, and susceptible to inference, takes a little longer to remind himself that Madeleine and Gersbach are not child murderers. In fact, the sphere of their sins, as Herzog comes to recognize, is the same sphere as his own—venial and potentially comic. "I sometimes see all three of us as a comedy team," Herzog tells Ramona, "with me playing straight man" (190). Moreover, Bellow's attribution of similar physical characteristics to both the mother who murders her child and to Gersbach subtly works to undercut the implied meaning of his own symbolic patterns. Red hair and gimpy legs, it turns out, really have nothing to do with diabolic behavior; Gersbach may look the part but he does not play it. It is literary and social convention that leads us to expect "fiery" or "passionate" or "short-tempered" or "violent" behavior from redheads. Of course we know better, but Bellow is perhaps subtly reminding us to remain skeptical of characterological explanations that are derived from stubborn conventions. Significantly, Herzog's most telling insight into Gersbach's character occurs only *after* he has stopped seeing Gersbach as extraordinarily malevolent and has allowed him back into the ranks of the fully human. "*Enjoy her,*" Herzog writes in a mental letter to Gersbach. "*You will not reach me through her however . . . I know you sought me in her flesh. But I am no longer there*" (318). To view Gersbach as governed by a latently homosexual need to cuckhold his best friend is an altogether more convincing appraisal of his character than the idea, promoted, if only to be undercut, by Herzog and Bellow both, that he is a devilish psychopath.

Some critics have read Madeleine and Gersbach as symbolic extensions of elements in Herzog's own personality and have therefore seen his coming to terms with them as an analogous coming to terms with what they stand for in himself.[44] It is true that part of Bellow's method of characterization is almost always to flank his protagonist with characters who do indeed symbolically extend his personality (a method that is of course recognizable as a pervasive tendency in literature; we might think of Hal flanked by Hotspur and Falstaff), it is hard, in the case of Herzog, to see quite how Gersbach and Madeleine represent Herzog's being. The closest that Herzog comes to exhibiting a Gersbachian trait is in his moral sentimentalism. Madeleine is sick and tired of the way in which Herzog idealizes his childhood and by inference criticizes his life with her: "Okay let's hear your sad old story. Tell me about your poor mother. And your father. And your boarder, the drunkard. And the old synagogue, and the bootlegging, and your Aunt Zipporah. . . . Oh, what balls!" (124). But what is primarily on display here is Madeleine's ruthlessness. Somehow the terms that define Madeleine's and Gersbach's characters do not seem appropriate to Herzog.

There is, however, a more interesting pattern to be discovered in the symbolic distribution of character in *Herzog*, one that we might call Cartesian. Throughout the novel, Herzog repeatedly expresses astonishment over the fact that despite his crisis he continues to remain in remarkably good physical health. The strength of Herzog's constitution works, as he says, "obstinately against his hypochondria" (12). Madeleine calls Herzog a "psychosomatic bully" (191), but although Herzog may occasionally acknowledge that he is or has been tempted to play the invalid in order to garner familial attention and sympathy, he never succumbs to the temptation. Herzog's healthy body, in fact, seems to signify that his mental equilibrium is perhaps not as disturbed as his antagonists like to make out. When Herzog repeats the opening line of the novel toward its end—"If I am out of my mind its all right with me" (1, 315)—the reader knows that what may have begun as genuine concern for his mental health has long ago subsided and that there is nothing particularly abnormal about the state of mind that Herzog is describing.

In fact, Herzog is surrounded by characters who are much crazier than he is. We need only to think of Sandor Himmelstein's plate smashing or Madeleine's uncontrollable shopping sprees. What is fascinating, though, is that an emotional alignment of secondary characters can be extrapolated in body/mind terms. Those who minister to Herzog's body are generally sympathetic individuals, but each such character has a counterpart who attempts to mess with Herzog's mind. Dr. Emmerich, who gives Herzog a physical, is professional, and as far as he can be, given that there is nothing wrong with Herzog, is sympathetic. Dr. Edvig, Herzog's analyst, is, by contrast, untrustworthy and manipulative. Herzog's "good brother," Will, helps to get him patched up after his car accident, while brother Shura, who is a shadowy figure in the novel, is seen to be engaged only abstractly with money and power. Ramona, as we have seen, is very concerned about Herzog's body (almost too much for Herzog's taste), while Madeleine, with whom Herzog has fraught and infrequent sex, directs her energies into elaborate strategies of deceit. Asphalter, Herzog's "good academic friend," gives Herzog booze and a bed for the night, while Shapiro has only intellectual battles to offer. What thus appears to be symbolically extended in the secondary characters is Herzog's mind/body split. His body remains healthy, as do his relations with those who cater to it; it is his mind that must battle with its own demons externalized analogously in the form of a group of antagonistic secondary characters. Emmerich, Will, Ramona, and Asphalter are "givens"—characters who will be there to support Herzog no matter what. Edvig, Shura, Madeleine, and Shapiro must be taken on and vanquished, and most important, their versions of Herzog's personality (are they right?) must be rejected.

It should be pointed out that the symbolic pattern that I am presenting intrudes into the text in only the subtlest of ways, and the secondary characters under discussion should not be viewed in simple black and white terms. All Herzog's sympathizers have their faults (Will's concern incorporates a misreading of his brother's plight and condition; he wants Herzog to enter a mental hospital "for his own good," and Herzog has to be careful how he behaves when in Will's company; Ramona lectures Herzog endlessly; Asphalter is eccentric), but their general attitude is sympathetic as are their personalities. Similarly, the cold-hearted Reality Instructors have their good points:

Shura is generous with his money; Shapiro has a fine mind; Madeleine has a compelling personality.

Some critics have suggested that Bellow is far more successful at animating his secondary characters than in giving a palpable "thereness" to his central figures (this charge is reviewed in the next chapter), but, oddly, critics have also complained that Bellow fails to endow his female characters with anything like the force and power that he gives to his central figures—who are always male. The reasons for this "dual reading" (which seems more than a mere difference of opinion) are to be discovered, where the secondary characters are concerned, first in the options for "fullness" or "roundedness" that the narrative point of view gives them and second in the ideological role that they play in the novel. Clearly, one of the problems in extrapolating secondary characters from *Herzog* is connected to the self-protective nature of the merging third- and first-person narrative. Madeleine, for example, like most of Bellow's women characters, can only play the role in the novel that she plays in the protagonist's life. She is girlfriend and wife but cannot be seen or understood as "student" or "colleague."

But there is a further charge, more serious, beyond the charge that we see only a limited picture of a secondary character, and this is that Bellow is a misogynist and that his misogyny manifests itself in the curtailed portraits of women that appear in his novels.

Does Bellow hate women? The distinguished critic Alfred Kazin described Bellow's *More Die of Heartbreak* (1987) as a work "fired by misogyny,"[45] and indeed the novel contains lethal portraits of manipulative women and charts in detail the protagonist Kenneth Trachtenberg's physical disgust with them. Unfortunately, it seems to me, *More Die of Heartbreak* is not really "fired" by anything. Bellow seems to be going through the motions, recycling his recent discursive prose and airing some of his less appealing prejudices in novelistic form. All novelists should be permitted their ups and downs, and we cannot be sure what prompted Bellow to give his hero such an ugly animus—the vicissitudes of his personal life perhaps or some desire to bait feminist critics who have attacked him. But whatever its roots, the publication of *More Die of Heartbreak* has revitalized the old arguments about Bellow's portrayals of women.

Herzog, in particular, carrying as it does the most elaborate portrait of a "bitch" in Bellow's canon (so many characters refer to Madeleine as a "bitch" in *Herzog* that the definition has begun to accumulate power long before we see Madeleine in action) seems open to interpretation as a misogynistic text. Madeleine is certainly cold, unprincipled, irresponsible, scheming, and manipulative, but she is not the only female character in the novel, and compared to her lover, Valentine Gersbach, she has a lot going for her. She is intellectually sharp, beautiful, and has a dramatic and inspiring personality. Female characters in *Herzog* are constrained in their development by the technical limits of the "protective" narrative in identical fashion to their male counterparts (with the exception of Herzog himself), but within these limits a variety of personalities nevertheless emerge who do not seem in any measurable degree to be "better" or "worse" than Bellow's secondary male characters. In *Herzog* there is none of the disgust with the female body and its functions that is latent in *Mr. Sammler's Planet* and explicit in *More Die of Heartbreak*. Rather than hating women, Herzog and Bellow both seem to be fascinated by women as emblematic of a larger theatricality to be perceived in the character of all.

In a revealing scene in *Herzog*, Herzog recalls the time that he has spent watching Madeleine get dressed and made up before she goes out in the morning. Herzog sits on the edge of an old bathtub in Madeleine's apartment taking in every detail of her preparations as if he were Alexander Pope observing Belinda at her dressing table. Herzog's intention, however, is not to satirize Madeleine's transformation of her face but rather to marvel at the intricacy and theatricality of the operation. Madeleine is a recent convert from Judaism to Catholicism, she also has a job teaching at Fordham, and she makes herself up with these two "roles" in mind. She wants to look severe enough to please the Monsignor who converted her and "sober and mature" enough to impress her university colleagues. To these ends, she puts on a carefully laid mask (quite literally) and dresses in the appropriate costume.

> First she spread a layer of cream on her cheeks, rubbing it into her straight nose, her childish chin and soft throat. It was gray, pearly bluish stuff. That was the base. She fanned it with a towel. Over this she laid the make-up. She worked with cotton swabs, under the hairline, about the eyes, up the cheeks and on the throat. Despite the soft rings of feminine flesh, there was already something discernibly dictatorial about that extended throat. She would not let Herzog caress her face downward—it was bad for the muscles. . . . She put on a pale powder with her puff. . . . She put touches of Vaseline on her lids. She dyed the lashes with a tiny coil . . . she put a touch of black in the outer corner of each eye, and redrew the line of her brows to make it level and earnest. Then she picked up a pair of large tailor's shears and put them to her bangs. . . . She primed her lips with waxy stuff, then painted them a drab red, adding more years to her age. This waxen mouth just about did it. She moistened her finger on her tongue, and brushed a few last touches on. That was it. . . . She put on a long heavy tweed skirt, which hid her legs . . . and a high necked sweater. . . . And now the hat. It was gray, with a low crown, wide-brimmed. When she drew it over her sleek head she became a woman of forty—some white, hysterical, genuflecting hypochondriac of the church aisles. . . . The job was finished. Her face was smooth and middle-aged . . . only the eyeballs hadn't been touched. . . . She put on a big pectoral cross. (111–12)

Madeleine, as has been noted, is an acting teacher's daughter, but her behavior in *Herzog* is not idiosyncratic. Ramona, who has less histrionic parents, also likes to get in costume; her wardrobe, though, is determinedly antithetical to Madeleine's, where Madeleine tries to look dowdy, Ramona goes for the exotic and erotic, "black lace underthings" and "spiked heeled shoes, three inches high" (203). "Her costume . . . it was a stunner" (204), says Herzog.

Female characters in *Herzog* go to extreme lengths (or what appear to be extreme lengths when examined under Herzog's careful scrutiny) to prepare themselves for the roles that they play, but for Herzog, all the world's a stage and men are equally recognizable as actors—their costumes and makeup are simply less extravagant.

Throughout the novel Herzog characterizes, with the wry smile of an appreciative but ironic member of the audience, the good and bad acting of the characters, both male and female, who surround him. Madeleine is endlessly theatrical, and Ramona mostly so; she particularly likes to play "the role of the tough Spanish broad" (16). The Monsignor who converts Madeleine is described as "an actor" with "one role, but a fat one" (112); Madeleine and Gersbach together are "grotesque love actors" (258); the participants in the various courtroom dramas that Herzog witnesses are "Actors all" (228). Herzog is also aware of his own thespian proclivities. The clothes that he purchases for his trip to Martha's Vineyard, a straw hat and striped jacket, could easily, as he himself notes, double as the costume for an old-time vaudeville performer: "And who wore such a hat, such a blazer? Why Lou Holtz, of course, the old vaudeville comic. He sang, 'I picked a lemon in the garden of love, where they say only *peaches* grow'" (175). The role of comic, foolish lover is one that Herzog sees himself most frequently as inhabiting. We have already seen how he regards himself, Madeleine, and Gersbach as members of a comedy team in which Herzog plays the straight man, but he also fantasizes marriage to Ramona—"Ramona in long gloves . . . introducing Moses with her charming lifted voice. . . . Moses, a different man, radiating well-being, swimming in dignity, affable to one and all"—as "a vaudeville show!" (202).

Is there a truth to human character beyond acting? At one point in the novel, as Herzog is preparing to go to Ramona's for dinner, he takes a shower and shaves before putting on *his* costume for the night. Standing naked before the shaving mirror Herzog tunes in his radio to some Polish dance music. As he shaves, the music begins to take him over, and Herzog finally "gives in for a while to the impulse to dance and leap on the soiled tiles." "It was one of his oddities in solitude," we learn, "to break out in song and dance, to do queer things out of keeping with his customary earnestness" (158). Here, then, is Herzog as the happy genius of his household, dancing naked just like the persona in William Carlos Williams's poem "Dance Russe." Herzog too, experiencing, as he does throughout the novel, the strange mixture of joy and desperation that permeates Williams's poem, might equally be singing "I am lonely, lonely. / I was born to be lonely, / I am best so!" The "naked" Herzog has something in him, some joy, that is not "reactive" in any way and that can transform a potentially unbearable loneliness into joyful solitude.

VIII

The "Problem" of Herzog's Character

We are entering on a thorny subject and one that I have thus far avoided—the essence, constitution, and construction of Herzog's character, a subject that raises the issue of Herzog's "thereness" or "presence" in the novel. The question "What kind of a literary character is Moses Herzog?" raises a variety of important issues, all of which have a bearing on a reading of the text as a whole.

Toward the end of Ralph Ellison's novel *Invisible Man* the narrator/protagonist finds himself meditating on the qualities and attributes of the conman Rinehart, a figure (almost a phenomenon) who possesses the ability successfully to disguise himself in any number of social roles.

> Still, could he be all of them: Rine the runner and Rine the gambler and Rine the briber and Rine the lover and Rinehart the Reverend? Could he himself be both rind and heart [by which I take Ellison to mean could he lay claim to an inner self, a core, while repeatedly altering his outward appearance]? What is real anyway? But how could I doubt it? He was a broad man, a man of parts who got around. Rinehart the rounder. It was true as I was true. His world was possibility and he knew it. He was years ahead of me and I was

> a fool. I must have been crazy and blind. The world in which we lived was without boundaries. A vast seething, hot world of fluidity, and Rine the rascal was at home. Perhaps *only* Rine the rascal was at home in it.[46]

As the invisible man is suspicious of fixed identities and promotes them in his own mind as imprisoning, Rinehart's multiplicity is appealing. However, Rinehart is also dangerously indefinable.

> You could actually make yourself anew. The notion was frightening for now the world seemed to flow before my eyes. All boundaries down, freedom was not only the recognition of necessity, it was the recognition of possibility. And sitting there trembling I caught a brief glimpse of the possibilities posed by Rinehart's multiple personalities and turned away. It was too vast and confusing to contemplate.[47]

Two quite different views of personality are mingled in these paragraphs. One of them, with which the novel engages, describes social identity, emphasizes its masklike qualities, and probes its artificiality. The other, from which both the invisible man and the novel "turn away," posits the essential fictionality of all being; in this formulation Rinehart's multiple personalities are analogous to the self's centerless and unceasing reconstitutions. Both these views of human personality seem to have been embraced although not necessarily endorsed by Saul Bellow: the first in Bellow's early novel *The Adventures of Augie March* (1953), where the hero's "identity problem" is engaged and plumbed; the second in *Herzog*, where, paradoxically in terms of the novel's governing impulses as I have thus far outlined them, Moses Herzog emerges as an incipient postmodern figure, a chameleon self whose quiddity, which he conceives of in transcendental terms, could equally be viewed as grounded in the rhetorical success or failure of the stories that he constructs about his life.

Like *Invisible Man*, *The Adventures of Augie March* is concerned with the ambiguous rewards of social identity. Augie, a free spirit, is contrarily drawn to anyone who has a plan for him; he is forever "giving himself up to other guy's schemes." Out of these schemes he emerges, usually dressed for the part, in a variety of social roles—gofer, paid escort, petty thief, huntsman/adventurer, bibliophile—none of which quite suits him. Augie is not quite sure who he is or what station in life he wishes to occupy, but he does know what he doesn't want, and the pattern of his relationships demands that he first embrace and then shrug off the identities that have been imposed on him. Augie's identity problem—he can define himself only in opposition, like that of Ellison's invisible man and that of his other contemporary unstable self, Thomas Mann's Felix Krull—is, I would suggest, symptomatic of a postwar malaise, a rupture in the general faith in consolidated character, a flattening of the salience of individual personality, what the critic Julia Kristeva has referred to as "the violently intense deflagration of psychic identity"[48] brought on by the mass killings and murders of World War II. For Kristeva, the psychic pain of the survivors and witnesses—anyone, in fact, who lived through those years and beyond—has remained mysteriously "invisible" and "unrepresentable."

In Saul Bellow's and Ralph Ellison's fiction there is no developed sense of the terminal misery of the postwar world, but there is a sense in which the "deflagration of psychic identity" is represented by their protagonist's failures to define themselves. What is unrepresentable, because it is no longer around, is not the "old stable ego" that D. H. Lawrence knew was gone after World War I but any self that is predicated on individual self-assurance or an overly elevated sense of self-worth. As Moses Herzog has it when reflecting on his father's misfortunes:

> What happened during the War abolished Father Herzog's claim to exceptional suffering. We are on a more brutal standard now, a terminal standard, indifferent to persons. Part of the program of destruction into which the human spirit has poured itself with energy, even with joy . . . So many millions—multitudes—go down in terrible pain . . . Personalities are only good for comic relief. (148–49)

It is no surprise given the contemporaneity of Augie March's allotropic social and psychological condition that some of the early reviews of that novel, while giving unreserved praise in most areas, nonetheless commented adversely on the "problem" of Augie's character. Robert Penn Warren, for example, wrote that "It is hard to give substance to a character who has no commitments" and added that the conception of the character might have been "stronger if Augie had been given the capacity for deeper commitments for more joy and sorrow."[49] What is surprising is that this critical position has largely been endorsed in Bellow criticism ever since, for the nature of the complaint is surely less against Bellow's supposed failure of characterization than against Bellow's vision of the self as endlessly theatrical, a vision that thus seems to contradict the endorsement of wholeness and selfhood that his novels otherwise seem to offer. Warren, if you like, was still working on the old standard, imagining that failure to give a conventional fullness of character to a protagonist was somehow a mimetic failure. I would argue that Augie is, in fact, a prototypical postwar personality. It is not that Bellow failed to give Augie character, but rather that Augie's character is a response to an altered conception of contemporary personality. As already has been noted, those characters in Bellow's novels who exhibit the richness and fullness that we conventionally demand are members, like Papa Herzog, of an older generation, and like Grandma Lausch or William Einhorn in *The Adventures of Augie March* or the old Jewish types who inhabit *The Victim,* they are altogether more confident and certain of themselves. The exchange between the old Yiddish journalist Schlossberg and two of his cronies in *The Victim* is instructive in this regard.

> "My mother sewed on her own shroud," said Kaplan. . . . "That's right it was the custom," said Benjamin. "All the old people used to do it. And a good custom too, don't you think so Mr. Schlossberg?" "There's a lot to say for it," Schlossberg replied. "At least they knew where they stood and who they were, in those days. Now they don't know who they are but they don't want to give themselves up. The last funeral I went to they had paper grass in the grave to cover up the dirt."[50]

The new postwar generation—Asa Leventhal's, Augie March's, Moses Herzog's—has lost touch with dread and death on a personal level while at the same time experiencing a historical assault on the individual of unprecedented indifference and brutality. The result, not surprisingly, has been a disintegration of solid notions of identity.

The exploration of the problem of identity—which became a keyword in the literary criticism of the fifties and sixties—with its emphasis on social instabilities and the individual's lack of "place," began to give way in the late sixties and early seventies to a far more radical critique of the cohesive self. The emergence of a group of postmodern writers—Pynchon, Barth, Barthelme, Gass, creators of tales "without plot or people," as William Gass puts it—coincided with the first structuralist and deconstructionist assaults on traditional notions of character in literature and selfhood in life. From the formulations and theories of Roland Barthes, Claude Lévi-Strauss, and soon after of Jacques Derrida emerged a vision of a deconstructing universe where notions of wholeness and selfhood were challenged and exposed and where the individual increasingly came to be regarded as a compendium of fictions constructed in our minds. However, the dismantling of character as an operative element in novels has not been confined to those postmodern writers who openly denigrate character but also includes authors of more traditional novels who embrace the idea of character in the larger themes of their novels and in their discursive prose—writers like Saul Bellow or Philip Roth.

The paradox can clearly be seen in *Herzog*. Bellow is a writer whose themes are definitely not the emptying out of the self and the loss of its meaning, nor do they appear to be the essential fictiveness of personality or the ambiguous transactions between fiction and life. As Daniel Fuchs discovered in the *Herzog* manuscript, Bellow's original intentions in the novel were forthrightly opposed to contemporary concepts of the self. "According to the latest from Paris and London," says Herzog, "there is no person. According to Bertrand Russell 'I' is a grammatical expression."[51] Herzog, of course, dissents. In Saul Bellow's novels we expect to find characters who are less stylized and far more present than those of his more experimental contemporaries and who embody the selfhood that in his discursive prose and in his novels Bellow seems to affirm.

Nevertheless, just as there were critics who protested the insubstantiality of Augie March's character, so too have there been critics who have pointed to the spectral qualities of Moses Herzog. "Herzog," wrote Tony Tanner shortly after the novel's publication, is "more of a presence than a person,"[52] while Irving Howe has described him as "not in the traditional sense, a novelistic character at all."[53] However, it seems that Herzog is very much "there" as a character, but he is there in uncompromisingly postmodern terms: he is in fact a compelling version of the contemporary personality, a self-creating figure who, as Herzog describes himself is an "industry that manufacture[s] personal history," (3) "a mind [that] observes its own personality . . . without approval" (12), or a character who "inflames [him]self with [his] own drama" (208). As we have seen, what this self-reflexive Herzog wants, finally, as he acknowledges to Asphalter, is to "change it all into language" (272), to self-consciously translate himself and those with whom he comes in contact into a restorative story.

In this light, Augie March's filling of a series of conflicting social roles as he endeavors to discover his true self appears as an early paradigm of Herzog shifting his modes of discourse while he attempts to become the author and thus the master of his own personal history. Herzog tries to tell the story of his life in such a way that all the angles will be covered, so that in his "constructions" he will be able to exert a control over himself and his many antagonists that he cannot exert in life. To this end Herzog writes mental letters, indulges in parodic self-analysis, projects his inner life onto the outer world, entwines memory and fantasy—all in an attempt to rewrite his experience into an acceptable form, a form that will lend meaning to his life. As he tells Asphalter:

> What can thoughtful people and humanists do but struggle toward suitable words? Take me, for instance. I've been writing letters helter-skelter in all directions. More words. I go after reality with lan-

> guage. Perhaps I'd like to change it all into language, to force Madeleine and Gersbach to have a Conscience. There's a word for you. I must be trying to keep tight the tensions without which human beings can no longer be called human. If they don't suffer they've gotten away from me. And I've filled the world with letters to prevent their escape. I want them in human form, and so I conjure up a whole environment and catch them in the middle. I put my whole heart into these constructions. But they are constructions. (272)

In the self-contained world of his own "constructions"—fictions, really—Herzog cannot be violated. But even in these ideal circumstances no single "version" of Herzog's story seems satisfactorily to engender the self that Herzog wishes and needs to inhabit if he is to emerge in health from the ruins of his marriage. Herzog is forever seeing through his own rhetorical devices, offering himself and us versions of himself from which he then withdraws, and it is in this sense that his mind observes his personality "without approval." Herzog "note[s] with distaste his own trick of appealing for sympathy" (12); or, having fabricated himself as a kind of environmental survivalist, adds, "he saw through this as well" (128); or, characterizing himself as "docile and modest," quickly notes, "he didn't deceive himself" (129).

The slides in the third-person narrative in and out of Herzog's consciousness seem to reinforce our ambivalent sense of Moses Herzog's cogency as a character and of his "knowability" as a self. The hinted presence of an all-knowing, extradiegetic narrator is suggestive of an all-knowable character and by extension of a knowable, definable self—the kind of centered being that Herzog would like to affirm is still possible to become. As he acknowledges, however, modern character is so far gone—is "inconstant, divided, vacillating," and, like Herzog's description of his own character, "cut off at times from both facts and from values" (107)—that it is only through transcendent intimations, like the one toward the end of the novel that Herzog experiences in the telegraph office, that we may imagine ourselves more than the "constructions" that it pleases us to call our lives. "Go through what is comprehensible," says Herzog, "and you conclude that only the incomprehensible gives any light" (266).

On the surface it seems as if in *Herzog* Bellow has thus subverted his own ideas of what constitutes worthwhile selfhood: where the text on one level endorses an optimistic notion of selfhood—a notion we derive from Herzog's insistence that "man somehow is more than his 'characteristics,' all the emotions, strivings, tastes, and constructions which it pleases him to call 'My Life'" (266)—on another it adumbrates the character of Moses Herzog in less certain terms. However, it seems that a double paradox is at work, for despite the fact that a sense of Herzog's motivational center remains elusive, Bellow has managed to create an engaging, complex, and compelling contemporary figure. If Herzog is a "presence," he is so perhaps only in the sense that we are all "presences"—impersonators capable, like Herzog, of playing the vaudevillian or the vengeful lover or even of imitating ourselves.

This view of human personality is neatly formulated by Philip Roth in *The Counterlife* (1986): "If there even *is* a natural being," says Nathan Zuckerman, "an irreducible self, it is rather small, I think, and may even be the root of all impersonation—the natural being may be the skill itself, the innate capacity to impersonate. I'm talking about recognizing that one is acutely a performer, rather than swallowing whole the guise of naturalness and pretending that it isn't a performance but you."[54] Herzog is certainly aware, as we have seen, of the performances that are given by others: Madeleine, Gersbach, Himmelstein, and so on. But what about himself? Is Herzog not also giving a performance? The answer is yes, but Herzog is giving us something else as well, for unlike the other characters whom the narrative does not give the opportunity to tell their stories, Herzog is giving us, in as variegated a manner as consciousness permits, the story of his life. And what a story it is, for whatever the root of the stirring energies released by Herzog's personal crisis—repressed violence against Madeleine and Gersbach, sublimations deriving from his sexual wounds—the eruptions in Herzog's mind are wondrous to behold.

Herzog's open narrative, where such a variegated world is created and which is symptomatic of his "open-self," comes in fact to represent not only an alternative to the one-part players with whom he is surrounded (Edvig, Himmelstein, Gersbach, Madeleine)—those all-knowing, absolutist authoritarians hiding behind their Reichian shields—but also a resistance to fixed ideas and absolute systems of belief that the novel as a whole endorses. Herzog in this sense may be viewed as a more sophisticated and intellectual version of the con men who exert such a fascination for Bellow—and for Ellison. One can assume fairly safely, I believe, on the basis of Saul Bellow's 1956 interview with the con man Yellow Kid Weil, that when Moses Herzog describes the Chicago bank robber and genius of escape Willie "The Actor" Sutton as "testing the power and completeness of all human systems" (177), it is an effort with which both our protagonist and his creator sympathize.[55]

What Bellow admired in the Yellow Kid was his resourcefulness, energy, and imagination, his genius for role-playing and for self-projection. But there is something else at work in Bellow's fascination with con men that bears on the characterization of Moses Herzog. Con artists and their cons, tricksters and their trickery are an important part of our literary heritage. Herman Melville, Mark Twain, William Faulkner, and Nathanael West all turned their attention to the operator, flim-flam man, or confidence man well before the type was taken up by Ralph Ellison and Saul Bellow. The unvarying function of such a character is to affirm, through the sophisticated rhetoric at his command, the provisionality of whatever value or belief we might wish to assert is stable or fixed—including, perhaps most important, the trust that we put in language to do an accurate job of translating our experience of the world.

The con men in Saul Bellow's novels fall into two categories, both of which derive from traditional characterizations of the trickster as sophist. On the one hand we have the demonic "tricksters" like Dr. Tamkin in *Seize the Day,* who brings Tommy Wilhelm to his knees by talking him around to making some foolish investments in the commodities market but who meanwhile has taken a cut out of what he knows to be the last of Wilhelm's savings, or like Dr. Layamon in

More Die of Heartbreak (Bellow has a penchant for charlatan doctors), a heartless wheeler-dealer scheming a marriage for his daughter to an unworldly botanist because he hopes to finagle a killing in downtown real estate out of the botanist's family connections. On the other hand there are the hieratic tricksters, like Mintouchian in *The Adventures of Augie March* or Dahfu in *Henderson the Rain King*—characters whom, while their genius for persuasion rests "on doubtful underpinnings," nevertheless impart messages that, initially anyway, appear to have real import and value for the protagonists who are in their thrall.

Inevitably, whether demon or priest, the hidden agendas of the con man/tricksters are revealed to the hero, at which point he severs his ties. However, the persistent presence of such characters in Bellow's novels and the mutual exigencies that evolve from the symbiotic relationships of the tricksters and the tricked suggest some singularity of purpose. The legacy that the con men deposit in the heroes' consciousness is perhaps an uneasy suspicion that the real con game is language itself. Bellow is not a postmodern game player strutting his stuff on lexical playing fields, but his heroes, propelled by their uncovering of the easy manipulations of language to which they have fallen victim, are often led to affirm their faith in a transcendent world beyond words, a world of the silent soul.

Characteristically, con men themselves are often deeply suspicious of language and with good reason, for more than anyone they are aware of the Machiavellian uses to which it can be put. In Thomas Mann's *Confessions of Felix Krull, Confidence Man*, for example, the protagonist at one point remarks,

> Only at the two opposite poles of human contact, where there are no words or at least no more words, in the glance and the embrace, is happiness really to be found, for there alone are unconditional freedom, secrecy and profound ruthlessness. Everything by way of human contact and exchange that lies between is lukewarm and insipid; it is determined, conditioned, and limited by manners and social convention. Here the word is master—that cool, prosaic device, that first begetter of tame, mediocre morality, so essentially

> alien to the hot, inarticulate realm of nature that one might say every word exists in and for itself and is therefore no better than claptrap. I say this, I, who am engaged in the labor of describing my life and am exerting every conceivable effort to give it a belletristic form.[56]

Krull comes to rest in an essentially Nietzschean position in which any and all use of language is viewed as persuasive rhetoric (in his formulation, "claptrap"). Although Bellow's protagonists certainly do not wish to affirm the "hot, inarticulate realm of nature" as supernal to language, they do tend to yearn for the cool, inarticulate world of the soul.

Toward the end of the novel, Herzog interrupts a letter to his late colleague Dr. Morgenfruh (a name that, as Harold Bloom has pointed out, is doubtless a Yiddish version of the Nietzschean Dawn of Day) to remark of his correspondent, "He was a splendid old man, only partly fraudulent, and what more can you ask of anyone?" (320). In Bellow's novels even the best of characters are partly fraudulent; sometimes, as in Morgenfruh's case, they are done in by a seemingly inescapable sentimentality, but sometimes the fraudulence seems to be an almost inevitable side-effect of being a talking animal. Herzog "goes after reality with language" but remains aware of the limitations.

In the world of words, of course, some people are much bigger frauds than others, and Herzog does his best to construct in language as close an approximation as he can of his experience. Ultimately, however, he puts his faith in fleeting but powerful transcendent experiences (like the one in the telegraph office) that hint at the existence of an authentic wordless self. It is no accident that at the conclusion of *Herzog* we find him stretched out on the Recamier couch in the study of his Berkshires house with "no messages for anyone. Nothing. Not a single word" (341).

There is another group of characters that frequent Bellow's novels, and although its members appear to come from an opposite corner from the tricksters/con men, in fact, they have a con game of their own going. In *The Adventures of Augie March* they are called "Destiny Molders" or "Imposers Upon"; in *Herzog* they are classified as "Reality Instructors." These characters generally claim, like Einhorn in *Augie March*, to be able "to show you what could be done with the world, where it gave or resisted, where you could be confident and run or where you could only feel your way and were forced to blunder."[57] For the Reality Instructors, a successful life in America can be achieved only through an unstinting manipulation of others; power comes through money and vice versa.

The supposed rationality of the Reality Instructors is central to the authority that they assume. Whether it is the autocratic Grandma Lausch making the "rational" decision to send Augie March's retarded brother, Georgie, into a home, or old Dr. Adler in *Seize the Day* berating his son for being overly subject to the vicissitudes of his feelings, or Sandor Himmelstein dressing down Moses Herzog for displaying a terminal naivety in legal matters, the Reality Instructors present a solid front in confirming the ruthlessness of the world in which they operate and that they simultaneously promote.

In a way that sheds light on the rhetorical battles in his novels, Bellow's quarrel with the antagonistic characters that he creates can be seen as akin to Nietzsche's quarrel with Socrates (as Plato gives him to us). Like Socrates, the Reality Instructors usually attempt to elicit the truth of a situation via a carefully contrived encounter of their supposed wisdom with the "ignorance" of the protagonist with whom they are dealing. In Nietzsche's radical critique of Western philosophy Socrates himself is revealed as simply yet another wily rhetorician who scores points by sheer tactical cunning. Bellow's characterization of his Reality Instructors similarly exposes a fundamental will to persuade craftily disguised as rational knowledge of how the world turns. Lausch, Adler, Himmelstein, et al. claim to have a handle on absolute truths, but their behavior and the persuasive methods that they employ to achieve their ends often starkly contrast with the supposedly rational purity of their thought. Paradoxically for such a hard-headed group, the Reality Instructors (who are mainly comprised of Jewish professionals—lawyers, doctors, psychologists) are often sentimentalists, exponents of what Herzog calls "potato love," and they use their largely phony feelings to sucker their charges into seeing things their way.

> Forming his lips so that the almost invisible moustache thinly appeared, Sandor began to sing, "Mi pnei chatoenu goino m'artzenu." And for our sins we were exiled from our land. "You and me a pair of old time Jews." He held Moses with his dew green eyes. "You're my boy. My innocent kind-hearted boy."
>
> He gave Moses a kiss. Moses felt the potato love. Amorphous, swelling, hungry, indiscriminate, cowardly potato love.
>
> "Oh, you sucker," Moses cried to himself in the train. "Sucker!" (91)

Like many other Bellow protagonists before him and since, Moses Herzog finds himself involved with a wide range of controlling individuals who think that they know the world but who turn out to be no more reliable in their behavior or accurate in their perceptions than the intriguing but daffy con artists who comprise the other large segment of the dramatis personae in Bellow's novels. For Bellow's heroes the only complete escape from this mixed crowd of sophists is up into the higher spheres, a journey that can be taken with the help of Meister Eckhardt (*Mr. Sammler's Planet*), Rudolf Steiner (*Humboldt's Gift*), communion with plants (*More Die of Heartbreak*), or just plain old transcendental epiphanies, as in *Herzog*.

In a short essay Harold Bloom described the character of Moses Herzog as "a wavering representation" especially when compared to some of the subsidiary male characters. This seems true, Bloom goes on to say, of almost all Bellow's fiction where "a Dickensian gusto animates a fabulous array of secondary and minor personalities while at the center [there is only] a colorful but shadowy consciousness."[58] The reasons for this, in addition to those suggested in the last chapter, may well be connected to the quality of the discourse that is distributed to the secondary and primary characters. The discourse of Bellow's secondary male characters (the women, as we have seen, are a whole other issue) is almost always grounded in the comic and the vulgar. Personalities like Sandor Himmelstein (the heavenly name is clearly ironic) are obnoxious, but they are also amusing, vital, compelling, and entertainingly earthy; like that cruel, put-upon bigot Jason Compson in *The Sound and the Fury* Bellow gives his heartless archmanipulators "all the best lines." By contrast, the discourse of Bellow's primary characters is often quirky, abstruse, or sometimes, as any reader of *Mr. Sammler's Planet* or *The Dean's December* knows, just plain boring. Bellow has much more difficulty in animating his primary figures, especially after they have begun to identify themselves with the abstract, the transcendental, or the metaphysical. The secondary characters, because their register and their "lines" are more memorable, tend to lodge in the reader's imagination as more "real."

More Die of Heartbreak is especially instructive in this regard. Benn Crader, the botanist with the metaphysical leanings whose character receives the solid endorsement of both the narrator/protagonist Kenneth Trachtenberg and the novel as a whole, is not easily extrapolatable into a substantial personality. Part of the problem derives from the fact that Crader is told and not shown. Trachtenberg discusses Crader endlessly with enormous admiration, and we are privy to revealing conversations between the two men, but we can only take Trachtenberg's word for the richness, vividness, and general wonderfulness he ascribes to his Uncle Benn because it is never demonstrated to the reader.

What Trachtenberg finds exceptional in Crader is a metaphysical frame of mind that manifests itself in higher thoughts, but he is equally impressed by the facility with which Crader extracts himself from the pressure of destructive relationships with women. Crader is adept at the higher forms of escape—capable, for example, of skipping an oppressive marriage by removing himself both geographically (to Antarctica) and mentally (via plant communion). However, as Leon Wieseltier noted in his review of *More Die of Heartbreak*, "transcendence cannot be part of a plot, since it marks the end of plot itself,"[59] and Crader, who spends much of the novel eluding the pursuant world, in particular the machinations of his in-laws and wife, ultimately is doomed to elude the reader as well. By contrast, we receive Crader's father-in-law, the horrible Dr. Layamon, in all the grotesque comedy of his being—his oppressive knee-grabbing physicality, his greed, his humiliating treatment of his female hospital patients, and so on.

The problems of characterization that arise in *More Die of Heartbreak* from Bellow's concern with a character who would like to abandon the erotic and domestic battlefields for the contemplative life are present, but in a different and more intriguing form, in *Herzog*. What Moses Herzog escapes, along with the designs of those out to crush him emotionally and the systematized ideas of those who wish to overwhelm him intellectually, are the traditional delineations of character. Herzog simply does not add up in the conventional way, and in his case it is the escape from the chains of the self that seem to command Bellow's attention. By defining himself so variously—one moment he is trying to be "a *marvelous* Herzog who, perhaps clumsily, tried to live out marvelous qualities vaguely comprehended" (93) and the next he is telling Ramona, "I've tried to be a pretty mediocre person if the truth be told" (189)—Herzog evades definition.

That is why critics like Tony Tanner and Irving Howe, writing before the postmodern explosion, had so much trouble grasping Herzog's essence. Herzog is simply not the kind of conventionally rounded character that we might expect Bellow's more or less conventional narratives to generate. In fact, the incipient postmodern characterization of Moses Herzog, while unusually strong and engaging for a portrait of such a "dismantled" self, nevertheless appears to subvert Bellow's affirmations of a given self—a self with a soul, an essence that precedes existence—affirmations that in his early novels are partly implied through traditional modes of characterization but that in *Herzog* are grounded on pure faith alone, transcendental intimations.

It is tempting, of course, to "read Herzog's character in terms of his ideas, but as we have seen, the "core" Herzog does not seem to be constituted of his philosophical musings. Herzog does a lot of thinking on abstruse subjects, but he remains oddly detached from his "higher thoughts." In like fashion, the "core" Herzog is not to be located in the past either, for while his memories are recovered with love and tinted with nostalgia, they nevertheless revivify a time that Herzog feels is "his ancient past, remoter than Egypt." At this distance the past has the power to move but not to define the individual.

The autobiographical elements in Herzog's life have, however, served another purpose—to spawn speculation about the autobiographical nature of the novel. One way to characterize Herzog is to characterize him "passively" via our fantasies of Bellow's own life, to fill in the supposed lacunae in Herzog's personality with information that we may have culled about Bellow from newspapers, magazines, literary journals, television appearances, attended readings, gossip, and so on. However, unlike Corde, the protagonist of Bellow's recent novel *The Dean's December*, Moses Herzog does not seem either to invite or to be in need of such filling in. Whatever the overlaps between Herzog's life and Bellow's, Herzog's character remains reckless, free, and viable, whereas Corde, as John Updike has written, seems an unsatisfactory "stand-in" for Bellow, a character tied so closely to Bellow that he has no life of his own.[60] The vexed question of Moses Herzog's character can resolve itself in two ways. We can accept the definition that Bellow himself has offered recently, in which Herzog's center is clearly identified as his soul:

> But there is one point at which, assisted by his comic sense, he is able to hold fast. In the greatest confusion there is still an open channel to the soul. It may be difficult to find because by midlife it is overgrown, and some of the wildest thickets that surround it grow out of what we describe as our education. But the channel is always there, and it is our business to keep it open, to have access to the deepest part of ourselves.[61]

We also can read Herzog's personality as storied, centerless, comprised of many selves. This is not to say that he lacks substance but rather to accept Philip Roth's premise that the natural being is a performer. If the quality of the performance is the criteria by which we judge character then Herzog is an engaging, profound, and substantial figure. In Bellow's novel, though, there is perhaps no either/or. The novel asserts and declares for the first formulation but subversively and mischievously enacts the second.

Notes

1. Bellow, in *A Biographical Dictionary of Modern Literature: First Supplement,* ed. Stanley Kunitz (New York: Wilson, 1955), 72.

2. Foreword to Allen Bloom, *The Closing of the American Mind* (New York: Simon & Schuster, 1987), 14.

3. See, for example, "Chicago: The City That Is, The City That Was," in *Life,* October 1986, 21–27.

4. Foreword, *The Closing of the American Mind,* 17.

5. "The Silent Assumptions of the Novelist." Talk given at the First International Saul Bellow Conference, Haifa University, Haifa, Israel, 28 April 1987.

6. *The Dean's December* (New York: Harper & Row, 1982), 201.

7. Foreword, *The Closing of the American Mind,* 16.

8. Ibid.

9. See Walter Clemons, "The Quest Never Stops: A Conversation with Saul Bellow," *Newsweek,* 8 June 1987, 79. See also the comments of Bellow's protagonist Kenneth Trachtenberg in *More Die of Heartbreak* (New York: Morrow, 1987), 100.

10. *Herzog* (New York: Viking Press, 1964), 311; hereafter cited in the text.

11. Interview with Gordon Lloyd Harper in *Writers at Work: The Paris Review Interviews,* 3rd ser. (New York: Viking, 1967), 193–94.

12. George Eliot, "Hurtsog, Hairtsog, Heart's Hog?," *Nation,* 19 October 1964, 252.

13. *Dangling Man* (New York: Vanguard, 1944), 9–10.

14. Eliot, "Hurtsog," 254.

15. Julian Moynihan, "The Way up from Rock Bottom," *New York Times Book Review,* 20 September 1964, 1.

16. Ibid.

17. John W. Aldridge, "The Complacency of Herzog," in *Saul Bellow and the Critics*, ed. Irving Malin (New York: New York University Press, 1967), 210.

18. Richard Poirier, "*Herzog* or Bellow in Trouble," in *Saul Bellow: A Collection of Critical Essays*, ed. Earl Rovit (Englewood Cliffs, N.J.: Prentice-Hall, 1975), 85.

19. V.S. Pritchett, "King Saul," *New York Review of Books*, 22 October 1964, 4.

20. Tony Tanner, *Saul Bellow* (London: Oliver & Boyd, 1965), 87.

21. Ibid., 94.

22. Ibid., 89.

23. See Daniel Fuchs, *Saul Bellow: Vision and Revision* (Durham, N.C.: Duke University Press, 1984), 155–78.

24. Mark Weinstein, review of *On Bellow's Planet* by Jonathan Wilson, *Saul Bellow Journal* 5 (Spring–Summer 1986):66.

25. Tanner, *Saul Bellow*, 101.

26. William Freedman, "'The Truth Is Hard to Get At': The Uncertain World of Saul Bellow's Fiction." Talk given at the First International Saul Bellow Conference, Haifa University, Haifa, Israel, 27 April 1987.

27. Jane Howard, "Mr. Bellow Considers His Planet," *Life*, 3 April 1970, 57.

28. See Lionel Trilling, *Sincerity and Authenticity* (London: Oxford University Press, 1972), 39, 41.

29. Adrienne Rich, *On Lies, Secrets and Silence* (New York: Norton, 1979), 186.

30. Pascal, *Pensées*, trans. A.J. Krailsheimer (1966; reprint, London: Penguin, 1975), 58.

31. See Milan Kundera, *The Unbearable Lightness of Being*, trans. Michael Henry Heim (New York: Harper & Row, 1984).

32. Robert Boyers et al., "Literature and Culture: An Interview with Saul Bellow," *Salmagundi* 30 (1975):23.

33. Jo Brans, "Common Needs, Common Preoccupations: An Interview with Saul Bellow," *Southwest Review* 62 (1977):3–4.

34. Bellow, Foreword to *The Closing of the American Mind*, 15–16.

35. Harold Bloom, Introduction to *Philip Roth: Modern Critical Views* (New York: Chelsea House, 1986), 2.

36. Nina A. Steers, Interview with Saul Bellow, "Successor to Faulkner?," *Show* 4 (September 1964):36.

37. Ernest Jones, *The Life and Work of Sigmund Freud* (1957; reprint, London: Penguin, 1981), 45.

38. Ibid.

39. Bellow, "Literature," in *The Great Ideas Today*, ed. Mortimer Adler and Robert M. Hutchins (Chicago: Encyclopaedia Brittanica, 1963), 135.

40. Bellow, "Laughter in the Ghetto," review of Sholem Aleichem, *The Adventures of Mottel and the Cantor's Son*, in *Saturday Review*, 30 May 1953, 15.

41. Bellow, Introduction to *Great Jewish Stories*, ed. Saul Bellow (New York: Dell, 1963), 10.

42. Tanner, *Saul Bellow*, 89.

43. Irving Howe, "Odysseus, Flat on His Back," *New Republic*, 19 September 1964, 21.

44. See, for example, Robert R. Dutton, *Saul Bellow* (Boston: Hall, 1982), 133.

45. Alfred Kazin, review of *More Die of Heartbreak*, in *New York Review of Books*, 16 July 1987, 3.

46. Ralph Ellison, *Invisible Man* (New York: Vintage, 1982), 487.

47. Ibid., 488.

48. Julia Kristeva, "The Pain of Sorrow in the Modern World: The Works of Marguerite Duras," *PMLA* 102 (March 1987), 138.

49. Robert Penn Warren, "The Man with No Commitments," *New Republic*, 2 November 1953, reprinted in *Critical Essays on Saul Bellow*, ed. Stanley Trachtenberg, (Boston: Hall, 1979), 13.

50. Bellow, *The Victim* (New York: Vanguard, 1947), 255.

51. Fuchs, *Saul Bellow: Vision and Revision*, 158.

52. Tanner, *Saul Bellow*, 106.

53. Irving Howe, *The Critical Point* (New York: Delta, 1973), 123.

54. Philip Roth, *The Counterlife* (New York: Farrar Straus Giroux, 1986), 320.

55. Bellow, "A Talk with the Yellow Kid," *Reporter* 6 (September 1956):608.

56. Thomas Mann, *Confessions of Felix Krull, Confidence Man*, trans. Denver Lindley (Harmondsworth, Middlesex, England: Penguin, 1973), 73.

57. *The Adventures of Augie March* (New York: Viking, 1953), 67.

58. Harold Bloom, Introduction to *Saul Bellow: Modern Critical Views*, ed. Harold Bloom (New York: Chelsea House Publishers, 1986), 56.

59. Leon Wieseltier, "Soul and Form," *New Republic*, 31 August 1987, 38.

60. John Updike, *Hugging the Shore* (New York: Knopf, 1983), 256.

61. Bellow, "The Civilized Barbarian Reader," *New York Times Book Review*, 8 March 1987, 38.

Selected Bibliography

Primary Works

Books

The Adventures of Augie March. New York: Viking Press, 1953.

Dangling Man. New York: Vanguard Press, 1944.

The Dean's December. New York: Harper & Row, 1982.

Henderson the Rain King. New York: Viking Press, 1959.

Herzog. New York: Viking Press, 1964.

Him with His Foot in His Mouth and Other Stories. New York: Harper & Row, 1984.

Humboldt's Gift. New York: Viking Press, 1975.

The Last Analysis: A Play. New York: Viking Press, 1965.

More Die of Heartbreak. New York: Morrow, 1987.

Mosby's Memoirs and Other Stories. New York: Viking Press, 1968.

Mr. Sammler's Planet. New York: Viking Press, 1970.

Nobel Lecture. New York: Targ Editions, 1979.

Seize the Day. New York: Viking Press, 1956.

To Jerusalem and Back: A Personal Account. New York: Viking Press, 1976.

The Victim. New York: Vanguard Press, 1947.

A Theft. New York: Viking Penguin, 1989.

Articles

"Culture Now: Some Animadversions, Some Laughs." *Modern Occasions* 1 (1971):162–168.

"Getting through America." *Boston Review* 13 (August 1988):9–10.

"Some Notes on Recent American Fiction." *Encounter* 21 (November 1963):22–29. Reprinted in *The Novel Today: Writers on Modern Fiction*, edited by Malcolm Bradbury. Manchester and London: Manchester University Press and Fontana, 1977; Totowa, N.J.: Rowman & Littlefield, 1977.

"Starting Out in Chicago." *American Scholar* 44.1 (1974–75):71–77.

"The Writer as Moralist." *Atlantic Monthly* 221 (March 1963):58–62.

Secondary Works

Books

Bradbury, Malcolm. *Saul Bellow.* New York: Methuen, 1982.

Braham, Jeanne. *A Sort of Columbus: The American Voyages of Saul Bellow's Fiction.* Athens, Ga.: University of Georgia Press, 1984.

Clayton, John Jacob. *Saul Bellow: In Defense of Man.* Bloomington: Indiana University Press, 1968.

Cohen, Sarah Blacher. *Saul Bellow's Enigmatic Laughter.* Urbana, Ill.: University of Illinois Press, 1974.

Detweiler, Robert. *Saul Bellow: A Critical Essay.* Grand Rapids: Eerdmans, 1967.

Dutton, Robert R. *Saul Bellow.* Boston: Twayne, 1982.

Fuchs, Daniel. *Saul Bellow: Vision and Revision.* Durham: Duke University Press, 1984.

Goldman, Liela H. *Saul Bellow's Moral Vision: A Critical Study of the Jewish Experience.* New York: Irvington, 1983.

Harris, Mark. *Saul Bellow: Drumlin Woodchuck.* Athens, Ga.: University of Georgia Press, 1980.

Levy, Claude. *Les romans de Saul Bellow: Tactiques Narratives et Strategies Oedipiennes.* Etudes Anglo-Americaines 5. Paris: Klincksieck, 1983.

Malin, Irving. *Saul Bellow's Fiction.* Carbondale: Southern Illinois University Press, 1969.

Newman, Judie. *Saul Bellow and History.* London: Macmillan, 1984.

Opdahl, Keith. *The Novels of Saul Bellow: An Introduction.* University Park: Pennsylvania State University Press, 1967.

Porter, M. Gilbert. *Whence the Power? The Artistry and Humanity of Saul Bellow.* Columbia, Mo.: University of Missouri Press, 1974

Rodrigues, Eusebio L. *Quest for the Human: An Exploration of Saul Bellow's Fiction*. Lewisburg: Bucknell University Press, 1981.

Rovit, Earl. *Saul Bellow*. Minneapolis: University of Minnesota Press, 1967.

Scheer-Schaezler, Brigitte. *Saul Bellow*. Modern Literature Monographs. New York: Ungar, 1972.

Tanner, Tony. *Saul Bellow*. Edinburgh and London: Oliver & Boyd; New York: Barnes, 1965.

Wilson, Jonathan. *On Bellow's Planet: Readings from the Dark Side*. Rutherford, N.J.: Fairleigh Dickinson University Press; London and Toronto: Associated University Presses, 1985.

Interviews

Boyers, Robert T. "Literature and Culture: An Interview with Saul Bellow." *Salmagundi* 30 (1975):6–23.

Brans, Jo. "Common Needs, Common Preoccupations: An Interview with Saul Bellow." *Southwest Review* 62 (1977):1–19.

Breit, Harvey. "A Talk with Saul Bellow." *New York Times Book Review*, 20 September 1953, 22. Reprinted in *The Writer Observed*. Cleveland: World, 1956, 271–74.

Crosland, Susan. "Bellow's Real Gift." (London) *Sunday Times*, 18 October 1987, 57.

Epstein, Joseph. "A Talk with Saul Bellow." *New York Times Book Review*, 5 December 1976, 92–93.

Harper, Gordon L. "The Art of Fiction: Saul Bellow." In *Writers at Work: The Paris Review Interviews*, 3d ser., edited by George Plimpton. New York: Viking, 1967, 175–96.

Howard, Jane. "Mr. Bellow Considers His Planet." *Life*, 3 April 1970, 57–60.

Kakutani, Michiko. "A Talk with Saul Bellow: On His Work and Himself." *New York Times Book Review*, 13 December 1981, 28–31.

Nash, Jay, and Ron Offen. "Saul Bellow." *Literary Times* [Chicago] (December 1964):10.

Steers, Nina. "Successor to Faulkner? And Interview with Saul Bellow." *Show* (September 1964):36–38.

Collections

Malin, Irving, ed. *Saul Bellow and the Critics*. New York: New York University Press, 1967.

Modern Fiction Studies 25 (Spring 1979). Special issue on Saul Bellow.

Rovit, Earl, ed. *Saul Bellow: A Collection of Critical Essays.* Englewood Cliffs, N.J.: Prentice-Hall, 1975.

Schraepen, Edmond, ed. *Saul Bellow and His Work.* Proceedings of a symposium held at the Free University of Brussels (V.U.B.), December 10–11, 1977. Brussels: Centrum voor Taal-en Literatuurwetenschap Vrije Universiteit Brussel, 1978.

General Studies Containing Discussion of *Herzog*

Aldridge, John W. *Time to Murder and Create: The Contemporary Novel in Crisis.* New York: McKay, 1966.

Galloway, David. *The Absurd Hero in American Fiction: Updike, Styron, Bellow, Salinger.* Austin: University of Texas Press, 1966.

Guttmann, Allen. *The Jewish Writer in America: Assimilation and the Crisis of Identity.* New York: Oxford University Press, 1971.

Howe, Irving. *The Critical Point.* New York: Delta, 1973.

Josipovici, Gabriel. *The World and the Book.* London: Paladin, 1973.

McConnell, Frank D. *Four Postwar American Novelists: Bellow, Mailer, Barth and Pynchon.* Chicago: University of Chicago Press, 1977.

Solotaroff, Theodore. *The Red Hot Vacuum.* New York: Athaneum, 1970.

Tanner, Tony. *City of Words: American Fiction 1950–1970.* London: Jonathan Cape, 1971.

Wisse, Ruth R. *The Schlemiel as Modern Hero.* Chicago: University of Chicago Press, 1971.

Articles and Reviews

Cixous, Helene. "Situation de Saul Bellow. "*Les Lettres Nouvelles* 58 (March–April 1967):130–45.

Eliott, George P. "Hurtsog, Hairstog, Heart's Hog?" *Nation* 19 (October 1964):252–54.

Galloway, David. "Moses-Bloom-Herzog: Bellow's Everyman." *Southern Review* 2 (1966):61–76.

Kermode, Frank. "*Herzog.*" *New Statesman,* 5 February 1965, 200–01.

Moynahan, Julian. "The Way up from Rock Bottom." *New York Times Book Review,* 20 September 1964, 41.

Poirier, Richard. "Bellows to *Herzog.*" *Partisan Review* 32 (1965):264–71.

Pritchett, V. S. "King Saul." *New York Review of Books,* 22 October 1964, 39.

Richler, Mordecai. "The Survivor." *Spectator* 29 (January 1965):139.

Shulman, Robert. "The Style of Bellow's Comedy." *PMLA* 83 (1968):109–17.

Steiner, George. "Moses Breaks the Tablets." *Sunday Times,* 31 January 1965, 48.

Bibliographies

Cronin, Gloria, and Blaine H. Hall. *Saul Bellow: An Annotated Bibliography,* 2d ed. New York: London: Garland, 1987.

Lercangee, Francine. *Saul Bellow: A Bibliography of Secondary sources.* Brussels: Center for American Studies, 1977.

Nault, Marianne. *Saul Bellow: His Work and His Critics: An Annotated International Bibliography.* New York: Garland, 1977.

Noreen, Robert G. *Saul Bellow: A Reference Guide.* Boston: Hall, 1978.

Index

About the Author

Jonathan Wilson is assistant professor of English at Tufts University. He is the author of *On Bellow's Planet: Readings from the Dark Side*. In addition, he has written many articles and review essays on contemporary American fiction.

About the Author

Jonathan Wilson is assistant professor of English at Tufts University. He is the author of *On Bellow's Planet: Readings from the Dark Side*. In addition, he has written many articles and review essays on contemporary American fiction.